May your *Moments of Truth*
and *Moments of Trust*
lead you to *enduring* impact

ERIC BECKER

THE
LONG
GAME

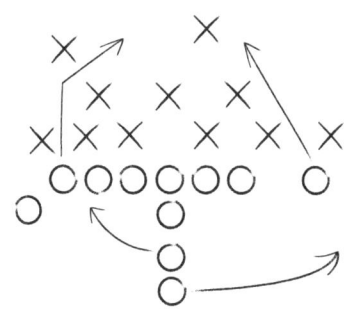

A *Playbook* of the World's
Most Enduring Companies

ERIC BECKER

RODIN BOOKS

Copyright © 2025 by Eric Becker

All rights reserved

No portion of this book may be reproduced in any fashion, print, facsimile, or electronic, or by any method yet to be developed, without the express written permission of the publisher

ISBN: 978-1-957588-32-2 (hardcover)
ISBN: 978-1-957588-33-9 (ebook)

PUBLISHED BY RODIN BOOKS INC.
666 Old Country Road
Suite 510
Garden City, New York 11530

www.rodinbooks.com

Book and cover design by Alexia Garaventa

Manufactured in the United States of America

To Jill, my partner in life and the long game. Your love means everything. Your smile and laugh make each day special.

To Jake, Greg, and Jen, our family is the greatest gift I could ever hope for.

To Cara, we miss you every day and have learned that love outlasts everything.

To Avy, the rarest of partners: visionary, values-driven, relentlessly committed to building a long-term multi-generational business for our clients and team.

CONTENTS

Foreword by Avy Stein _____ 1

Introduction: The Long Game _____ 5

1: Future Founding _____ 11

2: Mythbusting Mindset _____ 29

3: Moments of Truth, Moments of Trust _____ 45

4: Centurion Culture _____ 57

5: Ethos of Expansion _____ 71

6: Beyond Brand Affinity _____ 87

7: Super Stewards _____ 103

8: Ethical Succession _____ 119

9: Relationships Are Everything _____ 135

10: Time Horizons _____ 151

Epilogue: You Are the Next Cen _____ 165

Acknowledgments: What the Future Holds __ 175

FOREWORD

My favorite picture of Eric shows him as a young father, with his wife Jill and their three young children. He is holding a whiteboard while conducting a family meeting to discuss their family mission, vision, and values. His oldest, Greg, is around twelve years old and listening intently. To me, that photo captures the essence of Eric Becker. He sees the world with a vision for the long term, and he wants to empower the people around him to thrive.

It is an interesting juxtaposition. Eric and I came from long careers in private equity, where we were taught, at the risk of sounding Shakespearean, to know your exit before your entrance. For a significant part of both of our careers, we executed on a well-known strategy: make an investment, improve its valuation as quickly as possible, and begin to set it up for sale. Our role was to make the company better, in a compressed period of time, so we could maximize the return to our investors. And while Eric and I achieved success for ourselves and our partners by following that model, we came to the conclusion that we wanted to build businesses for the long term, businesses that would grow and prosper long after our involvement.

For me, this view is informed by an analysis that I undertook toward the end of my private equity days. My team and I looked at the fifty businesses we had owned and sold and approximated the returns we would have achieved holding these businesses substantially longer. It was no great surprise to learn that holding the businesses for the long term, like the great industrial companies and substantial family offices, created better results. Despite conventional wisdom, we and our investors would have benefited from maturing those investments for the long term. Eric and I spent many hours discussing our views on long-term vs. short-term strategies.

Later, when Eric and I formed our wealth management firm, Cresset, we conducted even deeper research on the value of holding a business for twenty years or more versus shorter periods of time. We studied the amount of friction you can take out of an organization and how much better it is from a return on investment perspective if you commit to using a longer time horizon. Eric and I were never fans of "shot clock investing" to begin with, and now we had the research to back what we believed. The result was that after decades of successfully buying and selling over 150 investments in the aggregate, Eric and I committed to structuring our own business so that it would be fortified to outlive us. Cresset, our multi-family office and investment business, is on a 100-year-mission built on a legacy of our values.

The "plays" you will see in *The Long Game* are a direct reflection of the man I like to call, "the most curious human you will ever meet." As a business partner, Eric is driven by a desire to understand not just how something works but also examine every angle in order to make it better.

He possesses this perfect combination of uncompromising integrity and the ability to execute his strategies, always doing the right thing.

Because Eric spent years as a founder and has been behind closed doors in hundreds of boardrooms while mentoring countless founders from startup to scale, he has seen many potential pitfalls and coached a myriad of entrepreneurs through them. But what makes him extraordinary is that Eric has the vision to drill down and solve the most immediate issue while helping businesses reassess their priorities and strategies for long-term stability and value creation.

So, why were so many of these iconic businesses willing to share their experiences, moments of vulnerability, and most critical lessons learned? Because they know their stories are in the best hands. Eric has developed an impeccable reputation with leaders from around the world based on trust and a respect for wisdom. That quality is the secret sauce for any entrepreneur who is eager to take the insights that Eric has laid out here and create an infrastructure of strength that has the power to propel their businesses forward and beyond.

—Avy Stein
Founder and Co-Chairman of Cresset

INTRODUCTION
THE LONG GAME

Growing up, one of my strongest memories was watching my father work. He took me to his office every Saturday and I would sit quietly in front of his desk as he did everything possible to move his business forward. Even as a kid, I could feel the magic of experiencing someone build an idea from scratch. I never even got upset that it was the weekend, when I could be hanging out with my friends. I knew my dad was trying to spend time with me the only way he could.

Plus, as a Jewish kid from Baltimore, my dad had chosen a wildly unexpected career. For fifty-three years, Gordon Becker was known as the King of Christmas.

His company, The Becker Group, got its start when he was struggling to pay his way through the University of Maryland. As the first in the family to go to college, Dad no doubt faced immense pressure to not let anyone down.

It was there that he had the clever idea to hire his fraternity brothers to dress up like Santa Clauses and contract them out to local department stores. As word spread, my dad started hearing from regional shopping centers and, eventually, malls all over the country. It was a seasonal business, but for my dad a year-round labor of love. And his hard work paid off. For over five decades, millions of children who had their photo taken with Santa were likely sitting on a Becker Group Santa.

The business would eventually expand to include Easter Bunnies, the irony of which, once again, was not lost on our Jewish family. At the same time, my dad evolved his Santa business to include every aspect of Christmas decor, including licenses for Disney, Peanuts, and Hanna-Barbera and Sesame Street.

And I know my passion to uncover the exact principles of building a future-proof business stems from every success or challenge my father faced that I was lucky enough to absorb from the front of his desk.

My dad believed in bringing me (and eventually my younger brother) along for the ride. I will forever be grateful for the access he gave me. At fourteen years old, I was taking business trips with him, my first foray into the adult world of work. I saw him cultivate personal relationships that lasted a lifetime. His customers were family.

By high school, I was sitting in on strategy and leadership meetings. There, they talked about international growth, breaking into Mexico and Canada, even the nuances of licensing Christmas products to iconic entities like Disney, Sesame Street, and the Muppets.

It was exhilarating. While I knew, even then, that I wanted to forge my own path, I was thrilled to be a fly on the wall, listening and learning.

I'm sure in his mind, my father was hopeful that these experiences would help connect me more deeply to the business, and if they didn't, there would at least be a trusted voice in the succession if something happened to him. What they actually did was show me the scaffolding for the core foundations of a successful business.

And that includes the challenges.

Any child of an entrepreneur can relate to the cycles of scarcity and abundance we lived through. When times were good, Dad would have a nice new car and we would fly to Acapulco for vacation, and when business was down, we would be in a beat-up station wagon driving to Ocean City, Maryland, even though the home we left behind was short on furniture.

Even through those tough times, as a young boy, I believed The Becker Group had the potential to last forever.

But I was wrong.

I watched my father take his beloved company through a Chapter 11 reorganization because, I now realize, he didn't fully understand how to scale and manage the seasonality of his business.

My father was smart, admired, and driven, but he lacked experience, a business education and, most importantly, a mentor. In a world where nearly half of all businesses fail within the first five years, it's remarkable that he managed to carry his company for over half a century. By the early 2000s, mall developers began to shift their practices and consolidate, which slowed sales.[1] Despite decades of hard

---

[1] Matthew Wells, "The Economic History of the Shopping Mall—and Its Future (Yes, It Does Have One)," Federal Reserve Bank of Richmond, third quarter 2022, https://www.richmondfed.org/publications/research/econ_focus/2022/q3_economic_history; Emily Matchar, "The Transformation of the American Shopping Mall," Smithsonian Magazine, September 12, 2017, https://www.smithsonianmag.com/innovation/transformation-american-shopping-mall-180964837; Avery Hartmans, "The Rise and Fall of the American Shopping Mall," Business Insider, January 26, 2023, https://www.businessinsider.com/shopping-mall-rise-fall-timeline-1950s-to-today-2023-1.

work, my father didn't anticipate the downturn. As a result, he had to sell the company to save it. It's some comfort that The Becker Group is still in operation today, but I know it isn't the dream my father had for it.

Imagine the possibilities if he'd had a playbook, filled with the lessons of those who came before him, sharing their wisdom on how they built a business to endure for one hundred years and beyond.

While studying economics at the University of Chicago, I spent a lot of time dreaming up what kind of company I could start to be like my dad. Maybe not the Santa business, but something of my own. One day, I walked to the campus bookstore and bought a book on how to write a business plan. I borrowed some money from my mom, bought the first PC IBM ever produced and started my first company. My brother Doug and I launched Life Card, a business anchored by an optical memory card we invented that could store eight hundred pages of medical history. Doug was a high school senior at the time and decided to defer his acceptance to Harvard. He never went. Meanwhile, I dropped out of the University of Chicago just one semester before graduation.

As a result of that decision, my father sent me to see a psychiatrist. He thought the family was moving backward: One kid who'd gotten into Harvard wasn't even going, and the other wasn't going to pick up his diploma.

In our first session, I told my new psychiatrist, Dr. Logue about my business idea and said if I fell flat on my face, I'd go back to school and finish. After our fifty minutes were up, Dr. Logue turned to me and said, "Are you looking for investors?"

Since then, I've built or invested in about one hundred companies, including Cresset, which I cofounded with my great friend Avy Stein, and it now manages over $65 billion in assets. On our website, we proudly share our vision and purpose, which is to serve clients, as an employee-owned company, for over a hundred years.

In this playbook, we'll use the term *Centurions* to describe businesses that have stood the test of time—those that have survived and thrived for over a century. While the word traditionally refers to Roman commanders of a legion of one hundred soldiers, we're adopting it to signify companies with enduring strength, resilience, and strategic longevity. Much like the Centurions of old, these businesses have not only weathered the storms of change but have emerged stronger, offering lessons that are as relevant today as they were a hundred years ago. Throughout this book, "Centurions" will be our reference point for businesses that embody the principles of long-term vision and adaptability.

While pouring myself into my own ventures, I continuously defined and redefined what I saw as the key components required to build a company that goes the distance. My passion has always been how to build better companies and stronger teams. Now I am bringing that experience to help organizations to play the long game so they can thrive over one hundred years. But I knew my hypotheses alone weren't enough. I began interviewing executives from long-standing, renowned organizations to see if what I believed was true. What they shared with me has been a gift, a rare glimpse into the private strategies, struggles, and successes of some of the most enduring companies in the world.

Exactly the playbook I wish my father had had all those years ago.

Eric

CHAPTER ONE
FUTURE FOUNDING

»»»

THE PLAY: *Leverage the principles of the past to inform every aspect of the future.*

Businesses built for longevity are rooted in a founding story that retains a constant throughline between the past and the future.

By the time I reached my thirties, I was what many would call a serial entrepreneur. I thrived in a start-up environment, putting together the pieces of the puzzle and building strategies for scale and growth. At the same time, a new fascination was fueling my curiosity. It all started as I walked along the waterfront in my hometown of Baltimore. I grabbed a copy of the *Baltimore Business Journal* and saw a list of the oldest companies in Maryland and a feature on the then 190-year-old Loane Brothers. A tent-making and rental business today, it has roots dating so far back that you might say it's literally woven into the fabric of American history.

I was very excited as I read the article. My head filled with questions: How did they do it? What were their secrets?

I wondered whether the company's longevity was a quirk in this era of "build fast, sell faster." How did Loane Brothers endure?

As I read about the company, I imagined what it must have been like for its founder and sailmaker, Joseph Loane. I envisioned him gazing out over Baltimore's harbor, watching the clipper ships dwindle as steamships took their place. Who would need sails anymore? What would become of the hundred seamstresses under his employ? The uncertainty must have weighed heavily on him, just as the shifting tides of industry weigh on us today.

I was enamored with their sense of pride, their keen understanding of their customers, and their unwavering commitment to mentoring the next generation. But what really struck me was their capacity to understand critical moments of truth and adapt with precision. Their longevity is not simply the result of good luck but rather the convergence of the right timing, the right people, the right guidance, and so much more. Loane Brothers had to pivot to survive, before anyone knew what a pivot was!

When I decided to write this book, I made a list of businesses that I most wanted to include, and the sailmaker-turned-tentmaker from my hometown, who sparked my interest in organizational longevity, was number one.

I sat down with Bryan Loane, company President and sixth-generation family member to take the helm.

"What has been instilled in us as we grow into the business is that this is a way of life you're signing up for," he says. "There are no standard hours. Our tents are a part of some of the most important events in someone's life, and you can't just deliver it and hope for the best. You have to be there and look after the details for every single client."

When he was a teen, his father stressed the importance of college but told him to major in what interested him.

"My father knew he would teach me everything I needed to know about running the business, particularly the intangibles, just as his father taught him."

Bryan credits Loane Brothers' longevity, in part, to its ability to pivot its product to meet the times. In 1815, Joseph Loane launched the company by selling custom sails to ships from Smith's Wharf, then known as the Baltimore Basin. After the Civil War, Loane Brothers was producing flags, tents, and covers.

"Whatever was needed or in demand, like flags were at the time," Bryan says, "Joseph Loane would sew it by hand."

Just as Bryan trained by working alongside his father, Joseph Loane's son Jabez began his apprenticeship a century earlier at the age of thirteen. Also one step ahead of the trends, Jabez is credited with fabricating the first window awning in the United States.[2]

In my years of working with successful multigenerational family businesses, I'm always gratified by the priority placed on mentorship and the collective spirit of celebration when a young leader makes their mark by accelerating the forward trajectory of the company. On the flip side, some founders are less generous with their support; they can experience cracks in the foundation when pride gets in the

---

[2] Bryan Loane (President, Loane Brothers), in discussion with the author, December 2023.

way of praise, impeding the chance of success for future generations. We'll talk more about succession planning in a later chapter.

Long-term companies like Loane Brothers have extra levels of care ingrained in their DNA, reflecting their distinctive integrity and attention to quality. And as Bryan says, that means going beyond the norm.

"When my grandfather cut fabric to make an awning, he always added an extra half inch of fabric, which gave the awning this little curve. Not because it needed it, but because it looked better, and he believed in giving his clients more than they needed. You can still see that signature style in our tents and awnings today."

Not only did this seemingly small touch have a big impact on the uniqueness of the product, the customer walked away feeling cared for by a business in an unexpected way.

That is how an organization stands the test of time.

» » »

Moses McKissack I—an enslaved brickmaker, carpenter, and father of fourteen—passed his craft down to his son Gabrielle "Moses II." Moses II, in turn, imparted the skills to his sons, Moses III and Calvin, who would go on to establish the company that continues to bear their family name and flourishes today.

While Moses I began practicing his trade in the early 1800s, it would take several decades before the third generation of McKissacks formalized the family legacy by incorporating the business.

CHAPTER ONE: FUTURE FOUNDING

Moses McKissack I was brought to the United States from West Africa and learned the craft of brickmaking from his enslaver, a prominent North Carolina contractor. Moses passed his trade to his ninth-born son, Moses McKissack II. Moses II became a master carpenter and built the storied gingerbread finishes on the Maxwell House Hotel in Nashville, Tennessee.

McKissack & McKissack, the nation's oldest minority- and woman-owned design and construction company, traces its founding to 1905. In 1922, Moses III and his brother Calvin achieved another historic milestone for the family and the nation by becoming the first licensed Black architects in Nashville.

"This was a family business that had been passed down for three generations before our founders incorporated us," President and CEO Cheryl McKissack Daniel tells me. "When they incorporated, they were working for homeowners, universities, throughout Nashville, much of Tennessee, Alabama, and some of the southeastern states."

The company's growth continued. In the 1940s, it went international, working on the newly established University of Haiti as part of an initiative to enhance educational facilities across the region. McKissack & McKissack served on building committees of President Franklin D. Roosevelt and made history in 1942 when the company was awarded a $5.7 million (about $107 million in today's dollars) contract to build the 99th Pursuit Squadron Airbase for the Tuskegee Airmen, the base for Black fighter pilots who fought in World War II.

As of 2025, McKissack & McKissack has planned, designed, and constructed more than six thousand projects, including renovating and constructing new buildings and additions to airports, universities, museums, and hospitals. Overall, the company has managed $50 billion worth of construction projects, including the new Terminal 1 at JFK International Airport, LaGuardia Airport's central terminal redevelopment, and renovation of the Coney Island Hospital campus.

Cheryl cites her fourteen years as an independent engineer for the city's Metropolitan Transportation Authority as a career cornerstone. Landing that contract, she says, set up McKissack & McKissack for transit work across the country as well as moving an MTA rail yard to make way for a massive Atlantic Yards development plan that included the Barclays Center, home of the Brooklyn Nets NBA basketball team.

In 2000, Cheryl bought the business from her mother (Moses III's daughter-in-law Leatrice) and moved the company headquarters from Nashville to New York City. There, she focused on building and leveraging the power of a diverse workforce and over a century of experience.

Despite the company's prominence today, Cheryl has never forgotten the legacy of her pioneering ancestors. Her Grandfather Moses III and Uncle Calvin faced the daunting task of "being two Black men building a business at the turn of the century."

That meant avoiding potentially deadly nighttime travel to visit out-of-state crews, where they would stay with family or friends because they weren't allowed in whites-only hotels and restaurants. "They would see their crews once a month. Can you imagine not being able to see your crew but once a month?"

CHAPTER ONE: FUTURE FOUNDING

I think about what this must have been like for them—extraordinarily challenging, marked by moments of immense joy, yet shadowed by fear and discouragement. This was not a level playing field.

There's more irony in the start-up of the pioneering McKissack & McKissack. The brothers built the town square in Pulaski, Tennessee, the city in which the Ku Klux Klan started. The Maxwell House Hotel, where Moses II had left his mark, later served as the site for the 1866 installation of a former Confederate general as the KKK's "Grand Wizard of the Invisible Empire."

"There are just so many dichotomies there that I often think about: What was it like?" Cheryl says.

That's why she honors her grandfather's motto, underscoring the challenges of those turn-of-the-century days: the four P's—persistence, perseverance, passion, preparedness.

"And my fifth one," she says, "is prayer."

Persistence, resilience, tenacity, and agility—these qualities are deeply embedded in the DNA of companies like McKissack & McKissack. Yet, few enduring entities have faced the kinds of challenges their founders encountered, challenges that were unique to their era and circumstances. Honoring those foundational triumphs is the legacy upon which Cheryl continues to build as she leads her business into the future.

Recognizing the strength of your founding story isn't just about honoring the past; it's about embracing the values that have carried you through adversity and leveraging them to navigate the future. These early victories serve as a blueprint, reminding leaders to stay grounded in resilience while adapting to new challenges. When a company holds onto the essence of its origins, it cultivates the tenacity and agility needed to thrive for generations, ensuring that the spirit of the founders remains a guiding force through every era of change.

»»»

THE PLAY: *Commit to exceeding expectations.*

Give people more than they imagine is possible. A vigilance for overdelivering is how reputations are born.

My wife Jill and I share a great love of travel. If you tell me the name of the most memorable place you've ever stayed, you can bet I am taking notes. So when we learned about the Castiglion del Bosco, a resort located on a world heritage site in Tuscany, Italy, we put it on our list and said, "Someday we will go." When we finally made the trip, the experience went beyond anything we could've imagined. Famous for its production of Brunello di Montalcino wine, the estate sits on almost five thousand acres of stunning vistas. One day, Jill and I went for a hike led by a hotel staffer who was mainly there to ensure that we were protected from the wild boars that roamed the forest near the property.

While walking, I became curious about the owners of such a magnificent property. The estate, as it turns out, was owned by the Ferragamo family, of the legendary Italian shoe and design dynasty. "How much is the family involved with this business?" I asked our guide.

"They are here every week," he said.

He told me how Ferragamo founder Salvatore instilled in his family what he called the "long eye." Salvatore's son Massimo, chairman of Ferragamo USA and owner of the

CHAPTER ONE: FUTURE FOUNDING

Castiglion del Bosco at the time, likewise possessed that trait. Our guide pointed to a terracotta-roofed building at least a mile away and noted that a tile was out of place. "Massimo can see that," he said. "He notices details others can't see."

And that is one of the founding principles of the iconic Ferragamo brand.

Salvatore was born in 1898, the eleventh of fourteen children growing up in the small village of Bonito, Italy. He knew early on that money was tight. So when his family couldn't afford new white shoes for his sister's first communion, a nine-year-old Salvatore borrowed nails, tools, thread, and canvas, and secretly produced his first custom pair. To the shock and delight of his family, Salvatore presented the shoes to his sister. The handcrafted pair was so admired, Salvatore became known as a young prodigy and was invited to learn the craft with a local cobbler. Salvatore's parents agreed, and a legend was born.

By age fourteen, after an apprenticeship in Naples, Salvatore had already opened his first small shoe store in his parents' home. His reputation as a passionate talent was growing, but at seventeen, he emigrated to Boston to join his brothers. He found work in a shoe factory and became fascinated by its modern machinery.

"Despite the intriguing new technology," James Ferragamo, Salvatore's grandson and Chief Transformation and Sustainability Officer, tells me during a rare sit-down conversation, "he also realized the manufactured shoe did not have the same quality as those that the artisans of Italy, like Salvatore, could make by hand."

This would mark the beginning of Salvatore's lifelong creative mission, forging a seamless marriage between what he described as "high tech and high craft."

In the 1920s, the footwear pioneer found his way to Hollywood, handcrafting shoes for the film industry. "He was constantly experimenting with cutting-edge designs, innovative silhouettes, colors, and materials that had never before been conceived," James says.

By the late 1920s, Salvatore had gained widespread notoriety and was creating shoes for some of the biggest movie stars of the time—Mary Pickford, Judy Garland, and Greta Garbo among them—earning him the title "shoemaker to the stars." Concerned about comfort as well as fashion, Salvatore relentlessly searched for ways to outdo himself. He even studied chemical engineering, human anatomy, and mathematics at the University of Southern California—all to modernize and reimagine his art.

When Salvatore died of cancer in 1960 at sixty-two, his wife, Wanda, then thirty-eight, decided to take over the business herself despite having no experience working in the industry—or working outside the home at all. But she, too, exceeded all expectations by looking beyond even her husband's vision and expanding Ferragamo into a global luxury goods brand.[3]

Can you even imagine what she was up against?

"I had never worked in my life before my husband died," she said in an interview for *Time* magazine. "I was a very young girl when I met him. At that time, women were

---

[3] Rachel Syme, "Wanda Ferragamo, 96, Dies; Reigned Over Family's Luxury Goods Empire," *The New York Times*, October 24, 2018, https://www.nytimes.com/2018/10/24/obituaries/wanda-ferragamo-96-dies-reigned-over-familys-luxury-goods-empire.html.

taught only to play the piano and paint and learn about culture. That's all."[4]

How provocative it must have been for Wanda to announce that she was taking that role—people surely assumed that she would fail, and fail quickly. But as we now know, the Ferragamo legend had only just begun.

At the time of his death, Salvatore had amassed over three hundred patents for his work, including the "stiletto" heel. Wanda, who passed away at the age of ninety-six, defied the odds and is now credited with scaling the business with intuition and the exacting standards that endure today.

With over $1 billion in revenue, the Ferragamo legacy has helped the company to rise from its humble beginnings to become one of the most recognized luxury brands in the world. To inspire new creative vision and manage its expanding portfolio, the business has expanded its leadership positions to include executives and designers from outside the family. This was part of a carefully executed succession plan that James detailed for me during our conversation; I will share it with you later in the book.

According to James, the brand continues to infuse its founder's vision and commitment to the craft while navigating the challenges of an ever-evolving global market.

"The legacy of my grandfather is an extraordinary gift," he says. "If you look through his designs, the archives, you realize so many of his shoes would still be considered modern today. They're full of special details. It's our desire to continue what he started and push it forward. To do so requires bringing in the right talent, creating a viable

---

[4] "Q & A with Wanda Ferragamo," *Time*, 2007, https://content.time.com/time/specials/2007/article/0,28804,1659346_1659344_1659299,00.html.

business infrastructure, and most of all honoring the past while keeping an eye on the future. One can't only live in the past; my grandfather wouldn't want it that way."

For Ferragamo, that means harnessing generations of exquisite craftsmanship with tech and innovation that supports the constant delivery of creative designs.

In 2022, Ferragamo made true on its vow to hire top executives outside the family, bringing in a new creative director, twenty-seven-year-old British phenom Maximillian Davis, who created one-of-a-kind Ferragamo looks for Beyonce's Renaissance World Tour.

The reputation of Ferragamo precedes their iconic founding story, always celebrating customers with a continuum of innovation built upon a legacy that laid the groundwork to reach its greatest potential yet.

》》》

In 1911, an aspiring entrepreneur named Louis Upton had a dream to improve the way we live. With his Uncle Emory and brother Fred, the twenty-two-year-old created the first washing machine powered by a motor.

Fred's son, Stephen, talked to me about the relationship between the two brothers.

"The beautiful part was that Uncle Lou was a real entrepreneur. He always had projects and plans and ideas. My father, Fred, was the stable force. He had a true head for numbers. They were a terrific pair."

In the early days, Louis and Fred set up their washing machines on the back of an old truck and drove around neighborhoods encouraging women to check out the invention. "And then they would encourage the women to talk about the washing machines over their backyard fences," Stephen says.

That grassroots tactic led Upton Machine Company to become the global enterprise known as Whirlpool, with $21 billion in annual revenue and seventy-eight thousand employees worldwide.

From the beginning, the Upton brothers were known to build their business based on a handshake and mutual respect.

"Quality and reliability were the cornerstones of the Upton philosophy," Stephen says.

One hundred twelve years later, Whirlpool Corporation is still considered one of the industry's most trusted brands and has been recognized by *Time* magazine as one of the world's best companies.

Dating back to its beginnings, the Upton Machine Company faced technical challenges and setbacks (more on that later) with its emerging products. But the foresight of Louis and Fred to put their invention directly in front of their potential customers is what sets them apart. By harnessing the excitement of women who up until this point, had been handwashing their clothes—and had probably never considered that someone would prioritize their time by creating something that improved their lives—the two men established an early example of true word-of-mouth marketing. And because they built a reliable product designed for ease, their rock-solid reputation strengthened for over a century.

As I have enjoyed a front-row seat to the ebb and flow of various performance indicators, identifying which ones matter most to the longevity of a business, certain pillars never change. Technology, social influence, competition—these are factors that will fluctuate. But integrity, dependability, and value—those are the qualities, when delivered with intention, that have the power to elevate your business from start-up to mainstay.

》》》

THE PLAY: *Cultivate a collective sense of purpose.*

It's the most satisfying feeling in the world to build a profitable business, but the companies that enter our souls are the ones whose purpose is greater than their product.

In the spring of 2023, a flurry of articles detailed how the brain of an entrepreneur is biologically different from others. These reports were based on a landmark study by Liège University Hospital and the University of Liège School of Management in Belgium. Researchers found that the entrepreneurial brain possessed what they called "cognitive flexibility," an ability to shift perspective, adapt to new information, and address problems in creative ways.

When I hear "cognitive flexibility," it's hard not to think about Carol Dweck and her cornerstone work on the growth mindset, the belief that intelligence and abilities can be developed through effort, learning, and persistence. The study out of Belgium, though researched through a different lens, validates what Dweck has been saying all along.

At Cresset, we constantly refer to "growth mindset" versus "fixed mindset." It's even included in our "culture card" that documents our values. I've always thought of the entrepreneurial mindset as a fascinating framework for life and problem solving.

Entrepreneurship, cognitive flexibility, growth mindset—they're all intertwined. They emphasize adaptability and resilience with the ability to pivot in the face of obstacles. This synergy beautifully captures the essence of entrepreneurial spirit. But sometimes it comes with a price. Studies also show that the intensity of building something from the ground up can cause higher instances of anxiety and mental health issues, like depression, among entrepreneurs.

The bridge between how we operate and how we feel—as opposed to how we think—might not be found in a brain scan; perhaps it's more connected to the heart.

Running a successful business can clearly take a toll. But if fostered in the right environment, it also has the potential to reward its founders and employees with a deeply shared experience of inspiration, satisfaction, and motivation. If employees can see that the work they do, at any level of the organization, is serving a greater purpose for the company as a whole, the meaning of both individual and collective success becomes richer.

» » »

One evening in 1912, a woman with an entrepreneurial, heart-led mission and vision decided to change the world.

After the death of her husband, Juliette Gordon Low was searching for a way to channel her boundless creative energy. Growing up in Savannah, Georgia, Juliette was precocious, confident, and clever. She was known as a creator of games and a leader of shenanigans among friends and family.

As an adult, Juliette was progressive and considered an adventurer for the times, pursuing her passions as an artist, a painter, and a metal worker. It was while visiting England in 1911 that Juliette met the founder of the Boy Scouts, British Army officer Robert Baden-Powell, and his sister, Agnes.

At the time, Agnes was leading a sister group to the British Boy Scouts called the Girl Guides. Juliette was so inspired by their work, she decided to lead two Girl Guide patrols herself in the UK and realized she had found her calling.

Upon her return to Savannah, Juliette immediately reached out to her cousin, Nina Pape, founder of a local girls school. It was during that conversation when Juliette famously said, "I have something for the girls of Savannah and all America and all the world. And we're going to start it tonight." What a declaration. Her vision, clear and unwavering.

On March 12, 1912, what we know today as the Girl Scouts of the USA was born.

"Juliette Gordon Low wasn't a person who heard the word 'no.' She believed anything was possible and there was a way to get anything done," says Shannon Browning-Mullis, the head of Girl Scouts of the USA Archives.

"And it's important to remember that this was a fascinating period in American history for women because so many were increasingly starting to think, 'We're not satisfied with some of the things in our community and in our country.' They're asking things like, 'What can we do about it? We don't have to stay home and wait for somebody else.' Juliette Gordon Low was one of these women."

The founding of the Girl Scouts of the USA coincided with an era of education reform, which focused on learning in the outdoors, teaching through games, and leading by doing.

This would form the principle tenets of the early Girl Scout ethos.

The first Girl Scout troop was composed of eighteen girls who, Shannon says, "all shared a sense of curiosity and belief that they could do anything." However, the girls were also realistic. It was 1912, and they were keenly aware of expectations and limited options.

Today, over fifty million women and girls worldwide have been a part of the Girl Scouts of the USA.

"One of Juliette's absolute principles was that the girls lead," Shannon says. "And so, whenever somebody would ask her what they should do in a given situation, she'd immediately put the scouts in a position of power and say, 'We have to ask the girls.'"

With that promise of empowering future generations, enduring legacies prevailed. The statistics are incredible:[5]

- Almost half of the current female NASA astronauts are Girl Scout alums.
- Fifteen of twenty-six female senators were once Girl Scouts.
- Eight of fourteen female governors were Girl Scouts.
- All three women who have served as secretary of state are either Girl Scout or Girl Guide alums.

---

[5] "Congressional Aide," Girl Scouts Nation's Capital, https://www.gscnc.org/en/members/events/congressional-aide.html.

Juliette Gordon Low set out to create what is now known as the Girl Scouts movement. And what she built has evolved into so much more.

I personally believe the annual Girl Scouts cookie sale is one of the greatest opportunities today for early entrepreneurship. In 2022, Girl Scouts of the USA reported revenue of $120 million, with all proceeds going back to the local council and troops to power experiences year-round.

When asked where this enduring organization might be in the next century, Shannon says, "How we build girls' courage, confidence, and character isn't the same as how we did it a hundred years ago, and it is not going to be the same a hundred years from now, but staying focused on those core reasons we exist, we'll find new ways to help support the strong leaders of our future."

From Juliette Gordon Low's earliest vision, the Girl Scout mission has towered above anything resembling profit margins or product development.

Is there a more clarifying mission than that?

I don't think so.

CHAPTER TWO

MYTHBUSTING MINDSET

»»»

THE PLAY: *Be agile and maintain a disruptive edge.*

Legacy organizations break stereotypes by operating with a great sense of clarity. They don't tolerate poor performance, and they don't sit on their laurels. They do have a sense of priority, importance, and timing.

Centuries-old businesses are often seen through an unfair lens. They're assigned generalized labels like "complacent," "too big to turn," or, most irksome, "resting on their laurels." I've found that nothing could be further from the truth. Businesses that persevere have a great sense of urgency. They have the gift of learning from their past, and know how to measure a threat and act on it swiftly. Though public perception might suggest otherwise, Centurion organizations have built agility and a willingness to take calculated risks into their longstanding formula for success.

Mention names like JP Morgan or Vanderbilt, and a common narrative emerges. These are entities rooted in the past, perceived to be resistant to change and slow to respond. Yet when we lift the veil and take a closer look, a different reality lies beneath.

Through generations of learning, their businesses have been built layer by layer with a solid, stable core but operate with a definitively disruptive edge. And as I discovered in my conversations with members of the Vanderbilt family, along with some of the oldest corporations in business, this approach has been encouraged since day one.

In 1810, local merchants in Hartford, Connecticut, pooled $15,000 to start The Hartford Fire Insurance Company.[6] Including "fire" in its title was no accident; fire was the era's predominant threat to life and property.

In the two-hundred-plus years since, the company now known as The Hartford has covered a wide range of individuals and projects: Abraham Lincoln and Babe Ruth; the construction of the Golden Gate Bridge, the Hoover Dam, and the Saint Lawrence Seaway. Their coverage has also spanned generations of disasters, like an 1835 fire that wiped out most of New York's financial district, the 1906 San Francisco earthquake, and the Great Chicago Fire of 1871, which left about one-third of the city in ruins and a third of the population homeless.[7] More recently, The

---

[6] "Hartford: Everything you need to know," *Insurance Business*, https://www.insurance-businessmag.com/us/companies/hartford/67011.

[7] *Britannica*, "Great Chicago Fire," last updated April 11, 2025, https://www.britannica.com/event/Chicago-fire-of-1871?utm_source=chatgpt.com.

Hartford paid out more than $850 million in claims following the September 11, 2001, terrorist attacks.

Despite those notable historic facts, the insurance business is among the least sexy in any field. You might assume that The Hartford, one of the oldest insurance companies in the nation, is among the stodgiest, the least likely to change its ways, the slowest to innovate. Think again.

Stilted language in insurance product titles got Laura Marzi, Chief Marketing Officer of Employee Benefits division, thinking about how they communicated with customers.

"Unfortunately," she says, "our industry is filled with insider language that helps brokers communicate to employee benefits decision makers, but doesn't really translate to the people who actually have to enroll in the coverage."

This particularly hit home when Laura and others were reviewing industry data that suggested people would opt out if they didn't understand the coverage. A staggering 85 percent of consumers they spoke with thought that the products being marketed *to* them weren't *for* them. At face value, they didn't understand the language.

"The people we spoke with were at all income levels and multiple literacy levels. And when we dug deeper, we found that there were stigmas. People told us they thought a product like life insurance was for 'rich people.' So why would they even want to buy it? What wasn't translating was that this product was basic coverage that could ensure final expenses are taken care of and that people don't incur more debt for their loved ones."

"Hospital indemnity" created "an incredible amount of confusion. Many of the folks we talked to said, 'Yeah, it's litigation insurance only for people who work at hospitals . . .' When in reality, it's cash that we pay you when you go into the hospital. It's for anybody who enrolls in it. So, those moments made me really sad but actually created a lot of motivation to change the narrative."

Revamping century-old language was a complex process with regulators, governments, and adjustments to meet legal and compliance standards, but it was worth it. "What was really cool is that we went back to the same consumers with a reframe of their products. We said, 'How do they sound now?' And we completely flipped it. Now, 85 percent understood what they were."

Just as life evolves, so too must the language we use to describe it. Listening to your customers and leveraging their feedback to inform innovation is not just a modern strategy but a fundamental aspect of enduring success. It is the antidote to being set in your ways.

》》》

With a rich history dating back to 1920, Isaia remains a premier name in Italian luxury fashion, today under the leadership of family successor and CEO Gianluca Isaia. He is renowned in his industry for his warmth, sense of style, and decadent advertising campaigns.

When I spoke to Gianluca on a video call, he sat behind his office desk in Napoli in front of a wall adorned with enlarged family photographs, wearing red, thick-rimmed glasses and drawing thoughtfully on his cigarette. Gianluca shatters the misconception that century-old businesses like his are rigid or outdated.

"We die every day, and we are reborn every day," he tells me. "And that's the key to being innovative, new, and fresh."

No matter how old your business, Gianluca says, you must stop and critically assess your product—even when things are going great.

"Sometimes I'll ask my tailors for something new or better, and they tell me how it's worked one way for thirty years. Why would they change it?"

Rather than settling for that answer, Gianluca challenges his tailors to do something different every day. And because of that, they are always working to make a better product than yesterday. This is Gianluca's disruptive edge.

Isaia was founded near Naples, Italy, by Gianluca's grandfather, Enrico, as a men's fabric store and tailoring company. Neapolitan craftsmanship was evolving into an industry leader in Europe and dramatically overhauling the approach to making men's suit jackets.

At the time, the traditional English jacket, in vogue throughout Europe, was too warm for the southern portion of the continent. Isaia's tailors were part of the movement to modernize the garment with traditional craftsmanship that discarded the inner lining and shoulder pads, using softer, lightweight fabrics. All of Isaia's collections are inspired by this style, but Gianluca vows the company will never stop innovating.

That philosophy was put to the test when the COVID-19 pandemic caused an unprecedented global shutdown in 2020. As people worldwide began working from home, the business suit was replaced with casual work attire—clothing just formal enough to make its wearer look put together for a virtual meeting. Comfort became a priority.

"You couldn't sell a jacket or suit for almost two years," Gianluca says. "We had a lot of people who didn't know what to do in the factory. I could have fired them. But instead, we internalized many categories that we were outsourcing before."

The company pivoted quickly. Sportswear, which had supplied only 20 percent of its sales, became Isaia's focus as Gianluca took back production from outside factories to make the merchandise in-house. They produced pieces that would supplement their signature suiting. Pajamas, robes, polo shirts, and jersey pieces became the priority.

In doing this, Gianluca saved numerous jobs. And as the world emerged from social distancing, he didn't face the staffing problems that so many others did. Many new companies panicked during the pandemic, laying off so many employees that when business eventually rebounded, they struggled to rehire talent and faced a shortage of available workers—a "great reckoning." The Centurion had outmaneuvered the new guys.

By retaining his talent and shifting company production into house-made sportswear, Gianluca made the business more profitable, reducing the amount of purchasing from other manufacturers and reselling.

Not only did it save the company, but suddenly, Isaia was positioned for growth. They were able to bring back their signature suits and other products when business picked up again, and they'd instilled in their tailors skills to showcase their trademark talents in new areas.

Gianluca also realized that as people came out of the pandemic and returned to work, a societal shift was still in play. Businessmen would likely resist reverting to the standard white-collar shirt and suit jacket. So he continued to pivot, adapting to the changing environment through innovation while safeguarding what the company stood for: expert tailoring.

By 2022, sportswear accounted for 40 percent of sales, twice the prepandemic amount. A challenge had become an opportunity, not a burden.

"And that's the key to being innovative," he says. "To be always looking for something new and fresh."

Gianluca exemplifies the agility needed to navigate change while honoring tradition. His commitment to continuous innovation underscores that true leadership is not just about preserving the past, but also about adapting swiftly to new opportunities, ensuring that the family business remains resilient and forward-thinking for future generations.

»»»

THE PLAY: *Differentiate perception from reality.*

Centurions know public impressions rarely match reality or intention. Even the most successful entrepreneurs and philanthropists experience financial setbacks. But as long as they stay the course—and remain open to the wisdom of others—they'll realize continued success.

It was at the iconic Biltmore Estate in Asheville, North Carolina, where I sat with members of the historic Vanderbilt family for a rare conversation. Together, we looked beyond the storied myths to understand the true origins of their Centurion legacy. Before it became a major tourist destination, Biltmore was simply "home" to George Vanderbilt and his descendants.

Our talk revealed to me how George, grandson of the shipping magnate Cornelius "the Commodore" Vanderbilt, was so inspired by the natural beauty of the land on his first visit to Asheville that he began building a fifteen-room country house to entertain family and friends away from the hustle and bustle of New York City. Shortly after, he assembled a team and committed a substantial portion of his inheritance to what is now the 250-room Biltmore Estate on the eight thousand beautiful acres where we were gathered.

Over time, George's vision grew from a family country estate to a bigger mission of preservation through self-sufficiency, a philosophy he embraced long before the first stone was ever placed. When construction began in 1889, an entire community of craftsmen came together to break ground on the largest undertaking in residential architecture in the nation.

Financial success would come later—so much later, in fact, that George's investment in the property resulted in a staggering annual loss of $250,000 for ten straight years. The first profit? A modest sixteen dollars.

I talked to Ryan Cecil, son of Biltmore CEO Bill Cecil, and Chase Pickering, son of Diana "Dini" Pickering, former Chair of the company board of directors and current Family Director. Ryan and Chase are the great-great-grandsons of George, who spent six years developing Biltmore, which was completed in 1895 and is now the nation's largest privately owned home.[8]

---

[8] Libertina Brandt, "Take a Look Inside the Largest House in the US—a Vanderbilt's 130-Year-Old Private Mansion with 35 Bedrooms, 43 Bathrooms, and 65 Fireplaces," *Business Insider*, April 26, 2023, https://www.businessinsider.com/largest-home-in-united-states-biltmore-estate-photos.

One of the most profound revelations in my conversation with Ryan and Chase was that people don't realize their great-great-grandfather, despite being a Vanderbilt, nearly lost everything trying to maintain the home.

"People often perceive the Vanderbilts and Biltmore House as symbols of wealth. But in reality, it was the opposite—it drained money. It consumed money," Ryan says, reflecting on the challenging early years that required hard work, meticulous planning, and unwavering faith in the long-term vision for the estate. George Vanderbilt was in it for the long game.

"He was just as concerned with drainage issues out in a field somewhere as he was with things like chandeliers inside the house," Ryan says.

Indeed, George wanted to create a luxurious country estate to entertain friends and family, but he was also dedicated to protecting this land for the future enjoyment of generations to come.

With his vision of a grand estate, George sought out Richard Morris Hunt to design and build the home, and landscape architect Frederick Law Olmsted to deliver on his vision of preservation and harmony with nature. Olmsted, who's best known for codesigning Central Park, was the perfect choice to bring this mission to life, and he encouraged George to do far more than build an opulent estate.

"It was Olmsted's recommendation to think beyond the big house to the contributions that he could make through an investment in western North Carolina, through agriculture and forestry specifically," Chase says.

To ensure the long-term health of Biltmore's vast woodlands, George enlisted Gifford Pinchot—who would later become the First Chief of the US Forest Service—to develop a forward-thinking forestry plan for the estate. Pinchot's work at Biltmore was revolutionary for its time.

Under his guidance, Biltmore's forests were managed not just for economic gain but for the long-term health of the land, ensuring that the estate's natural resources would thrive for generations.

"Biltmore would later become a national historic landmark—but it's not because of the big home," Chase says. "It's really because Biltmore is the birthplace of scientific forestry in America. Conservation started in western North Carolina through this great thinking."

George instilled a spirit of growth that led to further innovation throughout the twentieth century. His daughter, Cornelia, opened the estate to the public in 1930 with her husband, John Cecil, to boost tourism during the Great Depression while raising money to preserve the mansion. Biltmore stored priceless artwork from the National Gallery of Art during World War II. A winery was added in 1971, opened to the public fourteen years later, and still operates today. The family welcomed the new millennium by achieving George Vanderbilt's dream: The Inn on Biltmore Estate began hosting guests in 2001. Additionally, a gardener's cottage, built in 1896, was turned into luxury lodging, followed by a second hotel.

The idea for continuously reinvesting in the property set the groundwork for the business model they have today.

"Before we stepped into this role, our grandfather, Bill Cecil Sr., defined our mission for us, which is to preserve Biltmore Estate as a privately owned, profitable, working estate," Ryan says.

As the times evolved, so did the challenges, including the global pandemic and devastating destruction in the wake of Hurricane Helene that would bring area tourism to a standstill.

Much like Gianluca Isaia's high-end fashion falling short of demand during the COVID pandemic, the hospitality industry also took incredible hits. Biltmore faced a near total loss in revenue in the pandemic's first year. Many independent hotels ceased operations altogether, but Biltmore, like Isaia, was able to retain many of their employees by acting swiftly and decisively, recognizing the need for safe outdoor spaces and pivoting to serve customers in new ways. Their commitment to this new idea included lobbying the government of North Carolina for support and new legislation.

By diversifying the property while creating opportunities for long-term community and socioeconomic impact, Biltmore's consistent focus on agility and quick thinking has not only preserved George Vanderbilt's original vision but propelled it into the future.

»»»

THE PLAY: *Embrace disruption in order to discover a clear path forward.*

When faced with crises, the most enduring companies often unexpectedly choose the road less travelled. As long as you provide a clear map, you will find that humans are capable of incredible resilience.

A decades-long study by polling and data collection firm Gallup tracked companies' responses to major world events and disasters and noted that employees react to crises in two ways: with fear, helplessness, and victimization, or with self-actualization and engagement. Leadership drives which direction that takes.[9]

After decades of uncovering what the most enduring companies do to survive for the long haul, it's clear to me that you must empower your workforce with the right mindset to succeed amid calamity. A perfect case in point is Barnes & Noble. After starting as a single New York City bookstore in 1886, it grew to become the largest bookstore chain in the US, peaking in 2008 with 726 stores.[10] Customers reveled in the store's voluminous offerings and welcoming spirit. For a time, Barnes & Noble was the retail darling and for readers and analysts around the world; it could do no wrong. But the mammoth bookseller eventually fell on hard times.

After unsuccessful battles with online giant Amazon, Barnes & Noble was forced to shutter 150 stores, with more closings looming. Many thought the chain was doomed when it was sold in 2019 to hedge fund Elliott Advisors for $629 million.

Instead, the Centurion company brought in a new CEO, James Daunt, and supported his decision to unleash a surprising strategy. James began his tenure by giving authority and creative decision-making power to those at the bottom of the organizational chart.

Fresh from turning around Britain's largest bookseller, Waterstones, James presented a bold road map, disrupting

---

[9] Marco Nink, "8 Cultural Attributes of a Truly Agile Company," Gallup, November 20, 2023, https://www.gallup.com/workplace/544412/cultural-attributes-truly-agile-company.aspx.

[10] Amelia Beltrao, "Book Smart: Who founded Barnes & Noble?" *The U.S. Sun*, March 21, 2022, https://www.the-sun.com/news/us-news/4940348/who-founded-barnes-and-noble.

the conventional wisdom of prioritizing online sales. He proposed shifting to a business plan used by local independent booksellers: giving more autonomy to individual stores rather than imposing a top-down corporate vision. That entailed populating the stores with people who knew how to sell—and present—books.

"You've got to have a real passion amongst the team that runs that door," James says, "and you have to have a presentation of books that reflects the community in which you are. And if you do that, then you can get your customers."

Parlaying his deep understanding of what it takes to be a true bookseller, James deconstructed the company's training program and instead evaluated each employee's individual skill set.

"Most of the people running the stores were retailers," he says, "but they weren't booksellers. To be a very, very good bookseller is not easy. And just having resided in a bookstore, whether as a manager or as part of the wider team, doesn't turn you into a great bookseller, per se. You actually have to *be* one."

In other words, without equipping the right people with the right tools, true change isn't possible. For the fight ahead, James needed a uniquely qualified team in place—not great salespeople or marketers—but sellers of books.

"My strategy comes down to running really nice bookshops," he says, "and rejecting the 'sensible retailing principles' that make other bookstores inherently boring."

Gallup's research showed that when employees see agility at their company, they respond with their own agility. As a result, sales and customer satisfaction increase, and team members become more optimistic about their company's success. This translates to better performance, higher employee retention, and deeper engagement.[11]

"What you really have to do is lock in a culture that holds values central to it, and everything pivots around those values," James says. "I think that is what booksellers want. If you ensure that your central direction doesn't become corrupted in any way and holds to the same values, then, yes, you have something extremely powerful and enduring." We'll dive more into company culture later.

A business is as unique as a fingerprint, and at a young age, I realized situations can be transformed if you roll up your sleeves, learn the business's DNA, and then replicate it. This is what James was doing. "Reinvention" required his workers to be on board with his plan and be open to change.

He cleared the path for his booksellers and empowered them with an agile mindset. It was up to them to understand their business, leverage their community, and implement changes. Then they could deliver their products to market and stay ahead of the competition.

The strategy had an immediate impact. In 2024, after more than a decade of shuttering locations, Barnes & Noble opened more new retail stores than it had from 2009 to 2019, and announced plans for sixty additional retail stores in 2025.[12]

---

[11] "What Is Employee Engagement and How Do You Improve It?" Gallup, https://www.gallup.com/workplace/285674/improve-employee-engagement-workplace.aspx; Ed O'Boyle, "In Search of Agility," Gallup, March 12, 2024, https://www.gallup.com/workplace/611675/search-agility.aspx.

[12] Jennifer Mattson, "Barnes & Noble Will Open 60 New Bookstores in 2025, Breaking Last Year's Record As Bookstore Revival Ramps Up," *Fast Company*, February 3, 2025, https://www.fastcompany.com/91271622/barnes-noble-opening-60-new-stores-locations-full-list-of-cities-states-bookstore-revival.

It's interesting to consider the idea that what's old is new again—and it applies here to Barnes & Noble. James Daunt focused on returning to the fundamentals of what it means to be a great, authentic bookseller, and in doing so he rediscovered what made bookstores special. Instead of slashing costs or introducing radical new technologies, he looked to the past for inspiration and embraced traditional values that offered compelling solutions. Going back to the roots of what made the bookstore so appealing in the first place was a key element of its successful turnaround.

You must empower your workforce with the right mindset to succeed, even and especially amid crises. And it's just as clear that you must recognize the core truth of the issue—so you can act quickly to pivot away from it.

CHAPTER THREE

MOMENTS OF TRUTH, MOMENTS OF TRUST

»»»

THE PLAY: *Recognize a moment of truth.*

Those who are able to recognize defining moments, in both life and business, will be rewarded with outcomes far greater than those who cannot see the possibilities.

Jerome Monroe Smucker spent much of his life working his farm in Orville, Ohio. In 1897, he built a cider mill, feeding it with apples said to be from trees planted by John Chapman, better known as Johnny Appleseed, in the early nineteenth century. Before turning to its trademark business, Jerome made apple butter and sold it from the back of a horse-drawn wagon.

Today, the company has more than six thousand employees and an extensive reach into the food ecosystem beyond their jellies and jams. In 2023, for instance, Smucker's acquired Hostess Brands, makers of Twinkies, Ho Hos, and other snack products, for $5.6 billion. Smucker's ranked 465th on the 2023 Fortune 500 list with $8 billion in revenue.

That same year, the company reported that their signature ready-to-eat product for busy families, Uncrustables, generated $1 billion in annual sales, making it one of J.M. Smucker's top-performing brands. Its development involved meticulous attention to food safety and packaging, ensuring the sandwich was both nutritious and easy to store. Even after a century, Smucker's has been able to adapt and tap into consumer needs and market trends, transforming simple concepts into widely recognized and beloved products.

But in 1959, the J.M. Smucker Company faced a company-defining moment of truth: To keep the family-owned business in the hands of family members, they also would have to put it in the hands of the public.

The company was going to be hit with inheritance taxes upon the deaths of a few key family members. The amount threatened to devastate the overall health of the business. So, that year, Smucker's faced down its moment of truth, making the decision to sell one-third of its shares to the public and ultimately raising $2.3 million. The company's annual sales were $11.4 million, while earnings stood at $812,000. The risk paid off.

From that moment, the company began a ride that included acquisitions and expansions to make Smucker's among the giants in the food industry. Smucker's might be perceived as a quaint brand, making its homestyle spreads, but the reality is that it competes with the likes of ConAgra

CHAPTER THREE: MOMENTS OF TRUTH AND TRUST

and General Mills. Its catalog of brands includes Jif, Knott's Berry Farm, and Crosse & Blackwell, plus a range of pet food products (Milk-Bone and Meow Mix) and coffees such as Folgers and Café Bustelo. At the same time, scores of well-known competitors have come and gone.

I talked to Richard Smucker, Chairman Emeritus, who served as company President from 1987 to 2011, Co-CEO from 2001 to 2011, and CEO from 2011 to 2016.

"My grandfather really trusted the next generation to do the right thing with the business," Richard says. "And my siblings trusted my brother and me to run the company well."

Richard and his brother Timothy served as Co-CEOs, a practice not normally recommended for family businesses. "But we made it work," Richard says, "and we made it successful." Smucker's is a vintage American success story with all the trappings of a family business founded in the Midwest.

Even its famed slogan—"With a name like Smucker's, it has to be good"—has a backstory seemingly rooted in Americana. Paul Smucker feared the catchphrase, concocted in 1962 by a New York PR firm, might not resonate with customers, according to a 1987 *New York Times Magazine* story. He worried they could see it as demeaning of the small-town company, which hadn't done much advertising beyond word of mouth.

As the company president looked around the table of family members who composed the board of directors, he asked for opinions. One of them spoke up:

"Paul, do you think the slogan will help sell the jellies?"

"Yes, Aunt Winna," he replied, "I do."

"Well, then," she said, "it doesn't bother me."

The slogan, still used today, played quite well, and ushered in Smucker's rise to become the nation's number one maker of jellies and jams. "We're really all about managing and marketing brands," Richard says.

But that success didn't come without challenges.

For Smucker's, the company and shareholders have always come first. By the 1990s, Richard and Co-CEO Timothy engineered a series of acquisitions, further establishing themselves as industry leaders, but as the company profile grew, the family's stake in Smucker's was diluted from about 30 percent a decade prior to less than 6 percent. It was a big shift.

Deals with Procter & Gamble were structured as Reverse Morris Trusts, which meant P&G spun off its food businesses as independent companies, which in turn purchased 51 percent of J.M. Smucker. The deal was tax-free for P&G but required Smucker to issue new shares.

Richard explains his reasoning behind this decision: Retaining majority family control of the business was less important than ensuring they could retain key people. They needed to provide those people with continued growth opportunities within the company.

Recognizing this fork in the road, this moment of truth, allowed Smucker's to pivot and acquire new business. The strategy drove substantial growth, with major acquisitions in the 2000s followed by a half dozen smaller ones.

Smucker's transformative history extends far beyond simply creating new snacks; it's more about key strategic decisions that have shaped the company's trajectory. Their decisions to go public to manage estate taxes and, later, to expand through acquisitions that required them to adjust

CHAPTER THREE: MOMENTS OF TRUTH AND TRUST

ownership dynamics are testaments to recognizing critical junctures that can determine the future of a business.

Recognizing and navigating such pivotal moments is essential; overlooking them can lead to missed opportunities or unfavorable outcomes.

》》》

Founded in 1910, the Inés Rosales company survived a global influenza outbreak, a civil war, and an oppressive dictatorship. When democracy finally took hold in the mid-1980s, Spain's economy began to stabilize along with a growing competitive market. Nonetheless, in 1985 the classic torta company was on the brink.

"Consumers had walked away from the brand," Juan Moreno, President of Inés Rosales, explains, "because we had broken our contract with them." For seventy-five years, the Inés Rosales torta—a cross between a sweet cake and flatbread—was handmade with all-natural ingredients and the same custom packaging designed by the founder. The result was delivery of a consistently fresh and pristine product. But after a failed first attempt at expansion, the company pared costs by changing the protective packaging process that ensured the integrity of the torta. Consumers noticed the loss of quality, and sales began slipping.

It didn't take long for a vicious cycle to ensue.

I've seen many leaders ignore signs of pending disaster. It's like watching them careen headfirst into a brick wall, unable or unwilling to put on the brakes. They can't pivot from the problem because they haven't acknowledged that they are experiencing a critical moment of truth: Something is disrupting their path to success. It may be their business model, supply chain, economic challenges, technology failure, or, in Inés Rosales's case, a collapse of brand loyalty. When these clarifying moments happen, enduring leaders can see beyond the idealized vision of what they planned to achieve and be willing to do whatever it takes to fix the problem.

Confront your reality every day. When you do, great things can happen.

Juan Moreno had just taken ownership of Inés Rosales in the mid-'80s. He told me he knew immediately something drastic had to happen to rebuild trust with consumers who were used to a fresh, individually wrapped torta. But the shift to inferior packaging had caused sales to drop so low that the company was unable to purchase the original raw materials necessary to maintain the tortas' original quality.

Juan chose to risk everything.

He made the potentially catastrophic decision to recall every Inés Rosales torta from the shelves. It would nearly bankrupt the business, but Juan knew that without reestablishing the unspoken agreement between company and consumer, Inés Rosales would never survive. So they went back to the basics, reverting to the original, costlier packaging. The effort initially shrank their margins, but customers recognized that the tortas had recaptured their "original essence," as Juan puts it. "Sales exploded and capacity peaked." The company was once again thriving.

A similar quandary occurred in 2022. Olive oil prices skyrocketed,[13] and a decision loomed: Either substitute

---

[13] "Olive Oil Price Trend and Forecast," Procurement Resource, https://www.procurementresource.com/resource-center/olive-oil-price-trends.

lower-quality vegetable oil or maintain the implied pact with consumers. Inés Rosales once again chose to prioritize the integrity of the product at the expense of profit.

"Today, there has been an explosion of brands labeling themselves 'artisanal,'" Juan says. "Our competition can claim whatever they'd like. But at the end of the day, we know what we stand for. We know when we say 'artisanal,' we mean it. And our consumers trust it."

True leaders understand that trust is built not only on promises but on the consistent delivery of quality and authenticity that resonates with their consumers, especially in times of uncertainty. To maintain this trust, they must cultivate a keen awareness of the moments that define their brand's integrity and authenticity.

Recognizing these pivotal instances allows companies to pivot strategically, ensuring that their actions align with their values. In an ever-evolving marketplace, the ability to discern genuine moments of truth from mere trends is what ultimately distinguishes enduring brands.

》》》

THE PLAY: *Unite and sacrifice!*

Activate your bedrock during a moment of truth.

The Ferragamo family learned the importance of sacrifice in the face of a potentially disastrous moment of truth. After forty-eight years in business, skyrocketing inflation in the 1970s threatened to take out the famed shoemaker.

James Ferragamo explains: "At the time, the price of a Ferragamo shoe was eighty-five hundred lira [two hundred eighteen in today's dollars], but with inflation at eleven percent,[14] the shoe cost eleven thousand five hundred lira to produce." James's father, Ferrucio, and his uncle, Leonardo, had learned the importance of staying true to the craft from their father, the legendary Salvatore Ferragamo. But they knew they needed to take immediate action.

The brothers refused to implement cost-saving measures by reducing the quality of their handcrafted product. "But without a drastic move," James explains, "Ferragamo would fail." They agreed to put their personal savings back into the business. They asked other family members to do the same. "The family must unite and sacrifice" had been a founding principle established by Salvatore and his wife Wanda so many years before.

Knowing who your bedrock is, who you can count on, who is trustworthy, steadfast, and reliable, is invaluable when you're looking for support (we will dig into the "bedrock" piece more deeply in later chapters). For the Ferragamo brothers, it could not have been easy to admit they were facing a dire *moment of truth* and ask for both support and sacrifice.

Without questioning them, the family rallied to save the Ferragamo brand. This certainly wasn't the first time, nor would it be the last, but as James says, "Since its founding, the Ferragamos have understood what was at stake, and were willing to do whatever it takes to carry their business into the future."

When I think about the idea of "bedrock" in life and business, I'm reminded that in moments of great challenge,

---

[14] "Historical Inflation Rates: 1914–2025," US Inflation Calculator, https://www.usinflationcalculator.com/inflation/historical-inflation-rates.

CHAPTER THREE: MOMENTS OF TRUTH AND TRUST

we search for something solid to rely on. Initially, we might encounter things that seem dependable but aren't truly stable—they're more like quicksand than bedrock. But eventually we hit that solid foundation, and that's when we know we've found something we can genuinely count on.

»»»

THE PLAY: *Identify the next technological leap and evolve alongside history.*

The world is in constant flux—technology evolves, societies transform, and laws shift. What stands today is a world unrecognizable from a century ago.

In 1985, the convergence of two challenges brought about one of the most important pivots the world of electronic gaming has witnessed.

The seeds of the first electronic games, rudimentary simulations for computers or mainframes, were designed by computer scientists as early as the 1950s. In 1962, students at the Massachusetts Institute of Technology created *Spacewar!*, the first video-displayed game. From that point forward, the industry exploded.[15] Sales of home console systems led to a golden age of video arcade games—and a flood of competitive output. But an overabundance of poorly constructed and cloned games threatened the

---

[15] Chris Bateman, "Meet Bertie the Brain, the World's First Arcade Game, Built in Toronto," *Spacing*, August 13, 2014, https://spacing.ca/toronto/2014/08/13/meet-bertie-brain-worlds-first-arcade-game-built-toronto; Devin Monnens and Martin Goldberg, "Space Odyssey: The Long Journey of Spacewar! from MIT to Computer Labs Around the World," *Kinephanos*, https://www.kinephanos.ca/2015/space-odyssey-the-long-journey-of-spacewar-from-mit-to-computer-labs-around-the-world.

once-skyrocketing new vertical. The gaming industry was on its way to a crash in the '80s.

Meanwhile, a nearly century-old Japanese company, Nintendo Koppai, was about to make a series of pivots. Founded by craftsman Yamauchi Fusajiro in 1889, it was the purveyor of handmade *hanafuda*, or Japanese playing cards. For decades, the business dominated its industry. That is, until Yamauchi Hiroshi, the founder's great-grandson, traveled to the US in 1956 to visit a playing card manufacturer in Cincinnati. Disappointed by the card factory's size and scale, he confronted his first moment of truth: Playing cards had a limited future. At the same time, he knew companies like Atari and Magnavox were experiencing early success after creating gaming devices that plugged into the television. Hiroshi realized that the future was undeniably electronic toys.

Upon his return, Hiroshi encountered a line worker in his factory who'd designed a handheld mechanical arm extender. Yokoi Gunpei had originally been hired as a maintenance engineer, but after Hiroshi saw the mechanical arm, Gunpei was moved immediately to development and asked to replicate his invention as part of Nintendo's offerings. The arm extender can be used as a toy, but it's also commonly found today in hardware stores as a means to increase its user's reach.

This was the turning point for the playing-card manufacturer. Hiroshi officially shifted focus away from hanafuda production and launched a series of successful partnerships with other toy manufacturers, using Gunpei's electronic technology.

CHAPTER THREE: MOMENTS OF TRUTH AND TRUST

By the 1980s, just as global sales of video games began to stall, Nintendo struck gold.[16]

Gunpei was now heading up Nintendo's video game division, and Nintendo released Donkey Kong. Instantly, it was a smash hit. The game, featuring a barrel-jumping man with a mustache, would go on to become one of the most successful video games in history.

During his fifty-year tenure, Yamauchi Hiroshi transformed his family business into a global force in gaming. He stepped down as President of Nintendo in 2002. At the time of his departure, he said, "Coincidental to my leaving the company, I would like to make one request: that Nintendo give birth to wholly new ideas and create hardware which reflects that ideal."

The trick to identifying a critical moment of truth is to remain open to it. Stepping up to the challenge, like Atlas lifting the world with a lever, will yield profound results.

It's always obvious in hindsight, but the leaders who are able to recognize these defining moments will be rewarded with outcomes far greater than those who refuse to see the possibilities.

---

[16] "Video Game History," Smithsonian, https://www.si.edu/spotlight/the-father-of-the-video-game-the-ralph-baer-prototypes-and-electronic-games/video-game-history.

CHAPTER FOUR
CENTURION CULTURE

»»»

THE PLAY: *Create and define your culture from day one.*

Don't wait for your company culture to evolve on its own. Your team and the way it operates is an extension of the value systems you establish early and often.

Culture has become one of the strongest drivers of attracting and retaining top talent. While many benchmark businesses may not have prioritized it in the past, the most forward thinking have performed and acted upon "culture audits." They know culture is king. It's the DNA that powers every business decision, the shared norms, values, attitudes, and practices that form the companies' collective identity, the invisible glue that defines how their teams interact and perform.

It is relatively new for long-term businesses to layer culture into their strategy. References to "culture" in leading business publications leaped from fewer than five hundred thousand in 2019 to well over two million by 2021,[17] highlighting how crucial it is to understand what company culture is and how to shape it effectively.

If any one company can be cited for turning traditional corporate culture on its ear, it's Netflix, a business that started nearly thirty years ago as a DVD mailing service and quickly evolved into the streaming giant it is today.

From the start, Co-Founder Reed Hastings could see ahead to the future. He watched innovation accelerate at unprecedented speed. The team developing the logistical infrastructure and operations for shipping DVDs was the same group he would soon tap to shed that expertise and build a completely different entertainment experience from scratch. But how?

Along with his then Chief Talent Officer, Patty McCord, Hastings created the now famous culture deck in 2009, which former Facebook COO Sheryl Sandberg once called one of the most important documents to come out of Silicon Valley. It was a set of 127 unadorned slides—no music, no animation—shaping the culture and motivating performance at Netflix.

It worked. The culture deck created a stir with its bold, nontraditional approach. Prospective talent saw it as an invitation to be a part of something different. It allowed employees to do things like take as much vacation time as they felt was appropriate; it promoted radical transparency and talent density, retaining top talent even if it meant having fewer employees overall.

---

[17] *Global Culture Survey 2021: The Link Between Culture and Competitive Advantage* (PWC, 2021), https://www.pwc.com/gx/en/issues/upskilling/global-culture-survey-2020/pwc-global-culture-survey-2021.pdf.

CHAPTER FOUR: CENTURION CULTURE

The characteristics of Centurion businesses will forever evolve, and thanks in part to Netflix's deck, culture is undoubtedly one of the most important recent developments.

That said, there's a difference between talking about culture and being great at it. Recruiting, screening, onboarding, and retaining a world-class generational workforce continues to challenge organizations around the world. If ever there were a time to examine the culture and leadership practices of century-old businesses, this is it.

When Avy Stein and I founded Cresset in 2007, and before we brought on our first customer, we met with the first ten team members and told them, "We are on a one-hundred-year journey. Together." Our unique collective culture has been built since day one on protecting the integrity of our decisions to ensure that Cresset is here one hundred years from now. It's essential to us that every person who joins us is on board with that vision. We want to ensure that the next generation of our team is serving the next generation of clients and customers with the same core values.

After working with many businesses over four decades, I know there is no one-size-fits-all approach to creating a culture that attracts top talent and fosters employee engagement that serves the bottom line.

The culture of a medical research institution, for example, could have an element of seriousness to it—totally appropriate for an organization where lives may be on the line. Another culture might be equally as established, but with an element of fun, like Centurion toy maker Hasbro, whom I'll share more about in later chapters.

When employees understand and are aligned with their company's principles and mission, they're more committed to achieving the organization's goals and sustained performance.[18] Creating and implementing these foundational elements early on can be helpful in paving the way for the future.

That said, it would be unusual for a founder to craft a culture at inception and have it be precisely the culture you see one hundred years later. It's a bit more intangible—harder to define, and harder to pin down. Again, there's no one-size-fits-all recipe. While the paths to great leadership or other topics are more defined, culture can evolve in different directions.

I believe the brass tacks, if you will, in establishing a quality culture comes down to three key attributes: authenticity, repetition, and ownership.

Authenticity means the culture is demonstrated through actions—especially by the leaders, who set the tone for the entire organization. Employees and clients can sense when a culture feels contrived.

Culture is built through *repetition*. You can't simply issue a manifesto—like the "Cresset Culture Manifesto"—and expect it to automatically grow into the environment you envision. It's about identifying the core elements of your culture and then repeating and reinforcing them at every opportunity, setting a clear example and allowing others to see them in action.

I remember a company in which I served on the board, and the CEO, who was also the founder, fell seriously ill with cancer. This individual was highly respected and admired by his team. He instilled a sense of community that was felt from every level of the organization. He was

---

[18] "The Importance of Employee Recognition: Low Cost, High Impact," Gallup, June 28, 2016, https://www.gallup.com/workplace/236441/engaged-workplace.aspx.

the heart of his organization. Remarkably, the board, composed of individuals who were only meeting quarterly, stepped up in his absence. Though they weren't involved in day-to-day operations, they were inspired by the founder to pull together with a deep sense of commitment and care, taking on his weekly leadership meetings and guiding the company through a challenging period, until their founder returned. This was their culture in action.

The third key element is *ownership*. Our culture card says, "act like an owner." You have to own it! Whether it's a hospital caring for patients, a school with teachers educating students, or a company serving customers, personal accountability is a fundamental building block. Without it, there's no consistency, strength, or sustainability for the organization's longer term.

》》》

THE PLAY: *Be a team player and encourage an even playing field.*

You will foster greater success if the team views you as one of them.

Craig Freedman says that 130 years of culture at Freedman Seating Company continues to drive success through the company. He makes it his mission to lead in an empathetic way. "Obviously, we need to focus on our customers and our production, but really the foundation of our caring for our workforce is what's carried us all these years," Craig explains.

It helps that Freedman Seating is a family-run business where empathy appears to come naturally, but the reality,

Craig says, is that "there are only four of us who are really part of the ownership structure of the business. I think, though, our workforce and the people on the floor appreciate and enjoy the fact that the families include the managers, especially the higher-level managers."

Craig acknowledges that supervisors and owners who are also related can be a double-edged sword to nonfamily employees if "ownership sticks their head in, maybe where they shouldn't be, and making decisions or promises that we shouldn't be making without consulting them; that could be very frustrating and disruptive."

Freedman's motto encompasses what he calls his core culture tenants, the "three C's": communication, cooperation, collaboration. "Those are things we've been pounding home and instilling in our team and our people. And I think, for the most part, everyone in the company knows what those are."

Employees are not only invested in that philosophy, they're not afraid to make sure an owner is also accountable. "I love it when sometimes I'll get called out on it by somebody on the floor who might say, 'You know, you're not communicating.' And I'm like, 'You're right. Thank you very much.'"

That comfort level among employees "is what makes us a little bit different than other companies, especially in today's age with private equity and the expendability of employees."

Owners rolling up their sleeves, pitching in on the work, is noticed by the rank and file, Craig says. "That's what I continue to hear from them: 'If you guys are here, you're walking around the floor, you care.' That's what resonates."

I often talk about what we might call the Hamilton effect, or being in the room where it happens. It's something my father did exceptionally well, bringing my brother and me along in strategy meetings with his leadership when we were kids, letting us observe decisions (both good and bad), and helping us understand how to confront reality. That exposure was invaluable.

Craig Freedman deeply understands this transparent approach, seeded with respect—your people can quickly spot insincerity, and consistency between words and actions is crucial. It encourages learning, integrating other perspectives, and promoting the confidence to challenge the status quo or speak up.

I recall one such instance at Cresset when my chief of staff, around twenty-three years old at the time, was just starting at the company. During a big meeting she raised her hand, spoke up, and challenged something we had all previously agreed was the right course of action. Turns out she was right, and had we not listened, we may have faced a problematic outcome. It was great that even the youngest person in the room felt emboldened, empowered, confident, and comfortable. That confidence is something to foster, not quell.

You know your culture is working well when your people aren't afraid to speak up.

》》》

THE PLAY: *Follow the great examples set by your predecessors.*

Strong leaders leave behind the keys to their success through the culture they created.

William DeBerry McKissack (Cheryl's father), fourth-generation head of McKissack & McKissack, was known as a great connector. He had business associates in both the Black and white communities, formed strong relationships with politicians and other contractors, and collaborated on numerous projects, including construction of twenty Black colleges.

But in 1983, he unexpectedly suffered a debilitating stroke. Determined to keep the design and construction business in the family, his wife, Leatrice, stepped up to lead. Previously a stay-at-home mom, she faced immense pressure to sell the flourishing business under her husband's leadership. Instead, Leatrice rose to the challenge, proving she was more than capable of making tough decisions. Managers let it be known they were not accustomed to seeing women in strong leadership roles. So, with that, she cleaned house, replacing the senior management team "so they could appreciate the fact that she was running the business and not my father," says Cheryl McKissack Daniel, today's President and CEO.

Leatrice was well prepared and qualified to run the company. She had a master's degree in psychology, prior work experience, and the benefit of the McKissack family's prominence in the community. Cheryl shares, "The McKissacks' legacy as builders surviving enslavement filled within her the fortitude to keep the business in the family for the sake of her daughters."

The handoff occurred in 2000 when Cheryl bought the company from her mother. Today, she consults many in the industry for advice but tells me, "My mom was my early influence."

"I watched her build strong, genuine relationships with her clients," says Cheryl. "She would keep her word no matter the inconvenience—even drive six hours to meet a client, in person. She'd then sit with them, address all their construction issues, and take full responsibility for any problems. She would fix whatever was wrong and offer sincere apologies. Seeing her handle challenges with such grace and accountability had a profound impact on me and shaped the way I operate today."

The mentorship from her mom gave Cheryl at least one other insight. "I don't ask someone to do something that I personally couldn't do myself. And so, there are just certain principles that I learned from her that go a long way in building relationships."

These same relationships are expected to last. "We have legacy longevity. We plan to be around; we're just not going anywhere. And that's difficult when you think about how many businesses don't make it out of their first year, let alone five years.

"We take great pride in our legacy and the longevity of our company. But more than that, we are committed to doing the right thing. I strive to act with integrity to the best of my ability and ask the same of my staff. That integrity piece is critical—it's about over delivering and under promising. And we do a lot of that.

"Another thing is we have fun. We get together on a regular basis in social gatherings, and we don't take ourselves too seriously."

Cheryl adds that the company provides "a loose network" with guidelines while also encouraging employees to be creative within those guidelines. "We don't want anyone to be a robot, and some people don't work well in that environment."

But those who do thrive are "pretty much used to running their own little territories, almost having their own business within our business. They're free to make decisions, and if the decisions don't pan out to be good decisions, we talk about it. We figure out why, but we don't take away their decision-making authority or responsibility to the company. And I would say that's our culture."

As leaders, it's crucial to confront reality head on, acknowledging any deficiencies—whether they stem from complacency, miscommunication, or a disconnect between values and actions. Drawing inspiration from those who have come before us, we can identify the practices and principles that have nurtured successful cultures, allowing the business to survive.

Cultivating a vibrant company culture is not a onetime effort but a continuous journey of growth and adaptation.

》》》

THE PLAY: *Hire people who understand your culture and your mission.*

If your employees don't know what they're doing, how can they serve your customers?

Barnes & Noble was 122 years old when it achieved peak ownership of 726 bookstores in 2008. Nonetheless, just a few years later, it was teetering on the brink, closing 150 stores with more closures looming.

When James Daunt was named CEO in 2019, he quickly identified part of the problem: The company was

CHAPTER FOUR: CENTURION CULTURE

stymied by employees who were neither natural-born booksellers nor trained in the unique art of selling a book. The result was a less-than-rewarding customer experience. Well-known for his directness, James doesn't hold back when he explains what went wrong. "When I look at the complete mess that my predecessors made of this business, I think the biggest problem they have is they just don't understand it. They don't understand the people, and they don't understand the motivations. And it's mainly their lack of understanding of their own people, but it's also a lack of understanding of their customers."

The company ethos needed to do a 180.

"I came into a culture that was wholly absent of any performance management around standards and behaviors. Before I arrived, you'd only get fired at Barnes & Noble if you did something egregious. If you steal, for instance. You don't get fired for being a useless bookseller because that's not egregious.

"There was this pervasive mentality, 'Our store managers are fantastic. Our store managers are tenured at the beginning of time, and they are amazing.' And then suddenly you've got somebody, like me, turning up who's going, no. No. No. No.

"Some of you may be amazing, but I would like to know which of you are, because in my humble estimation, not a very simple estimation, you probably run the gamut from extraordinarily amazing and wonderful and brilliant to perhaps useless and potentially quite toxic."

His job, he says, was to spot the ones with potential, training them and "showing them what excellence is and making them great."

So, while James made the very public move of removing the previous top-down corporate structure, giving local managers increasing autonomy, he made sure to identify the managers who actually understood the unique and skilled nature of bookselling culture.

James has encouraged his newly trained managers to cultivate employees who truly understand and love to sell books. "I think the bookselling teams found what I was articulating easy to understand and quite gratifying because it seemed to be about devolving responsibility to them and equipping them to do their jobs better."

Another key to staffing bookstores is an awareness of the types of people who will excel in them. "Booksellers are quiet, introverted people. The nature of bookstores—they are very friendly and supportive environments—encourages that." And people, kids in particular, who love to read will thrive in such an environment.

"A business such as ours requires the full support and engagement of its employees. They need to respect, and be respected by, the owner."

What James has done is bold, and necessary. He's demonstrated that when a culture isn't a fit with the innate skills of the employees, the business suffers. It's critical for people to be able to see themselves reflected in the way a company culture has been designed. When that clicks, there is an almost instant sense of empowerment and belonging. Knowing who your employee is on their best day is what helps get you through your worst days.

》》》

CHAPTER FOUR: CENTURION CULTURE

In 2010, I ran a contest where I asked twenty current CEOs and eighty board members, most of whom were retired or former CEOs, "What is the best question you've ever asked or been asked?" The winner of that contest was a gentleman named Gary Keisling, a veteran CEO. He said, "Every day I ask myself, What am I tolerating but shouldn't be?"

I believe this is the greatest question in the world: What am I tolerating but shouldn't be?

When I think of the hundred or so companies I've been involved with in my career, just about everything you can imagine has happened to them: bad, incompetent, or unethical leadership; people making poor decisions; people just being unlucky. But the organizations that had the strongest cultures recovered, persevered, and thrived. They confronted their challenges and made the appropriate changes. That's the catalyst for growth.

The good news in all of this is, no matter what happens, you have every opportunity to fix your culture.

If there's something that's not working, the first way to fix it is to confront it. What am I tolerating but shouldn't be? I think that applies to your culture, business, and your life. Very much like James Daunt's approach at Barnes & Noble.

A strong culture protects the organization.

CHAPTER FIVE
ETHOS OF EXPANSION

»»»

THE PLAY: *Keep growing.*

When we are at our best, we are growing. The bitter truth about growth is that when you stop, it's the start of going backward, and shrinking has already begun.

The Second Law of Thermodynamics says if the physical process is irreversible, the entropy of a system must increase.[19] Entropy, of course, is associated with disorder or uncertainty. When measured in business, entropy means an organization begins to decay or decline without energy.

The healthiest organizations, much like the healthiest and happiest people, are the ones that are growing. Growth is a fundamental pillar, providing organizational energy. It creates opportunities for new hires with new ideas to join

---

[19] "Second Law—Entropy," *Beginner's Guide to Aeronautics.* National Aeronautics and Space Administration, Glenn Research Center. https://www1.grc.nasa.gov/beginners-guide-to-aeronautics/second-law-entropy/

the team, and for existing employees to advance into new roles. The experience can feel a little like getting out over your skis: You're at the edge of your ability, and you know you could fall, but it's also exhilarating.

But growth comes with an important caveat: You have to know how much to expand and also when to slow down. Sometimes you get the formula right, maybe you get lucky. But if you're in expansion mode too long, people start to burn out, mistakes are made, and things start to break.

The trick is to figure out how to grow at a sustainable pace, and when you're not growing, to recalculate: *Why are we not growing? Is our product or service outdated? Is our marketing outdated? Is our client retention not there?*

It often comes down to innovation or, more often, a lack thereof. In a 2024 study by Fast Company and Deloitte, 65 percent of the world's most innovative companies said that a focus on innovation is expressed in their mission, vision, or value statements and in their reporting structures.[20] And innovation drives growth. Today, it's technology and AI that are reshaping the way we think, build, and do business, and it's happening with unprecedented speed. But for our Centurion companies, reinvention has always helped drive expansion.

Polish-Jewish brothers Herman, Hillel, and Henry launched what was originally known as Hassenfeld Brothers in 1923. They started out by selling textile remnants, followed by pencil cases and school supplies. In the 1930s, the company tried creating modeling clay and nurse

---

[20] 2023 *Survey of Innovation Excellence: Deloitte Summary Report* (Deloitte Development LLC, 2023), https://www2.deloitte.com/content/dam/Deloitte/us/Documents/mergers-acqisitions/us-2023-innovation-survey-report.pdf.

and doctor kits for kids. It wasn't until 1952, after decades of testing and product innovation, that the Hassenfeld Brothers struck gold with a quirky toy called Mr. Potato Head. The little spud with interchangeable facial features may have seemed simple, but it set the brothers on a historic trajectory—including the creation of the first-ever television advertisement for a toy. In 1968, the company changed its name to Hasbro Industries, Inc., and in 1985 it officially became Hasbro, Inc.

Today's CEO, Chris Cocks, talked to me about the company's approach to innovation and diversification.

"I think the first thing is, know your center," he says. "Really know what the core of the company is. Whenever we've vectored away from it, we've tended to gravitate toward troubled waters. And whenever we correct ourselves, we always find our way back. And for us, our center is the power of play."

Hasbro and its brands are built on the belief that play is for everyone—a simple yet powerful mission statement that drives their economic engine. Using what they call "play patterns" as the lens through which they innovate, Hasbro has expanded their gaming and entertainment divisions with a relentless focus on diversification. The resulting robust product portfolio has allowed the company to ride out the good times and the bad.

"I think most companies that are around for over a hundred years aren't around for a hundred years by accident," says Hasbro CEO Chris Cocks. "They tend to have a growth mindset about new opportunities, disruptive technologies, and they try to adapt or adopt them rather than fight them."

Chris's predecessor, the late Brian Goldner, embodied this ethos of growth and expansion when he positioned the company to be one of the first to translate their intellectual property into movies. In the 2000s, then-CEO Goldner launched his crusade to convince Hollywood executives that action figures like Transformers—around since 1984—and G.I. Joe were film-worthy.

Goldner fulfilled much of his dream, but his contributions were cut short when he died in 2021 at age fifty-eight.

"Brian spent maybe five or six years working Hollywood to find someone to believe Transformers could be turned into a movie," Chris tells me. "He saw every wacky curveball you could possibly get thrown at you.

"At one point, the production executives at Paramount didn't want the robots to talk; they didn't understand why the hell anyone would want to listen to talking robots on the screen," Chris says. "But he was able to successfully find real believers in the project, like Michael Bay" (the director) "and Steven Spielberg" (the executive producer). "He was able to find allies inside of Paramount."

The venture's success was staggering, beginning with the release of the first Transformers film in 2007. At this writing, the franchise's seven films have grossed more than $5.2 billion. "It's spawned one of the top ten most popular movie franchises ever. And hundreds of millions of dollars of incremental profit and value for Hasbro's shareholders. So, certainly, that was a big one. And a seminal moment for Brian."

And then there are the risks taken that don't turn out as planned.

In 2019, Goldner oversaw the $3.8 billion acquisition of Entertainment One, a Canadian production studio that

CHAPTER FIVE: ETHOS OF EXPANSION

produced the popular children's series *Peppa Pig* and *PJ Masks*. This would allow Hasbro to produce its own films and shows rather than partnering with Hollywood studios.

Chris was only a few months into his tenure as CEO, but it was "clear that the integration of the eOne acquisition hadn't gone well. There was very much an us-versus-them mentality between the two sides. And the pandemic really threw the whole business model for a loop."

At a management off-site retreat, Hasbro's mission was discussed. "It was all about building joy and connectivity through the power of play. And everyone was gravitating toward it—except for the leaders of eOne," Chris says. "Someone with them had asked: 'How does this connect with eOne productions like *The Rookie* or *Naked and Afraid*?'

"That question hit me like a sledgehammer," he says. "The answer was: It doesn't. And the reason it doesn't is because the two entities don't belong together. It was a catalyzing moment of saying, 'We're gonna need to bite the bullet, and spin this off.'"

Hasbro took a significant loss on the sale of eOne, but it activated a return to center. Leadership took it as a powerful signal, both to the market and internally, that they take their principles of play seriously. And in this case, it was quite a fundamental epiphany about what belongs in the company and what doesn't.

When growth initiatives reflect the organization's values, they foster a sense of authenticity and trust among employees and customers alike. And when they don't, as in the case of eOne, recognizing that *moment of truth* and making a pivot can be critical to survival.

Expansion is fundamentally about creating opportunities and enhancing shareholder value. And a strong growth culture motivates your workforce, reduces turnover, and helps employees achieve their goals, encouraging them to stay with the organization.

Companies may experience periods of slow growth, which is acceptable after rapid growth or an acquisition. However, prolonged stagnation can lead to decline, a dangerous position for any organization. Understanding why a company isn't growing is vital for fostering a culture of growth and making long-term success possible.

Ultimately, meaningful growth should focus not only on financial metrics but also on resonating with the organization's foundational principles and its reason for being, ensuring that growth honors the mission and positively impacts stakeholders.

》》》

Since the early 1900s, Whirlpool Corporation has fostered growth while keeping "make life easier in the home" at the heart of its innovation and growth strategy.

The early iterations of Lou Upton's 1911 patented motorized wringer-washer originally didn't catch on, and he had invested his last $500 in his Upton Machine Company. But he believed in his invention.

"That was where he said, 'I lost everything, but I'm keeping this idea. I'm gonna electrify it and turn it into something that really gives people their time back,'" says Pam Klyn, Whirlpool's Executive Vice President of Corporate Relations. "And that ultimately is still at the core of everything we do, one hundred thirteen years later."

Whirlpool continues to focus on appliances and, perhaps inspired by Lou Upton's willingness to iterate, innovation remains a key to product improvement and sustainable growth. The company also has a long history of creative, grassroots marketing, dating back to when Lou and his brother Fred Upton brought their new wringer washer directly to the neighborhoods and demonstrated it where women were accustomed to hanging out their laundry by hand.

Fast forward to 2001, when Whirlpool rolled out the Duet, a front-loading washer and dryer set that boasted ease of use, extreme energy efficiency, and gentle fabric care. While this product hit all the marks innovation-wise, the strategy behind its launch was the standout.

Concerned about tipping off its industry rivals and having just made budget cuts, Whirlpool didn't advertise the product at launch. The Duet debuted at the Kitchen & Bath Industry Show, but rather than showing it at the venue, company leaders set up a private hotel suite across the street and invited editors of industry publications to take a break from walking the trade show floor and check out the intentionally unnamed Duet products.

Editors were given one-on-one interviews but required to sign nondisclosure agreements that limited how quickly they could publish their stories. The gambit to create intrigue worked: A follow-up showed that twenty-one of twenty-five editors present wrote about the Duet, giving it unprecedented free publicity.

"There's a ton of work in energy and investment. When we bring a new product to market or change a product, it's tens of millions of dollars to do this. So, it has to be very intentional," Pam says. And this extends to the innovation itself.

Whirlpool has always listened to and leveraged its consumers' feedback as key drivers for change. Today, company leaders implement satellite focus groups and ask for volunteers to install cameras in their kitchens and laundry rooms. This allows them to study real-life engagement with Whirlpool products and see how consumers deal with any design flaws.

The footage, Pam says, can be revelatory. One woman, for instance, was shown stopping her dryer five times to adjust the load—but she couldn't believe it until she saw the recording.

"None of us know our compensatory behavior," Pam says. "With these focus groups we get to watch which human behaviors are making up for what a product doesn't do or doesn't have. For example, people have no idea how often they kick the dishwasher door up to close it."

Observation of dishwasher users led to the introduction of a third rack, which provided 27 percent more capacity. "The dishwasher is exactly the same size because you have to fit it in that cabinet space, but no consumer would have said, 'Gee, I wish I had yet another rack.'" Customer feedback is used as fuel to innovate.

Whirlpool Corporation officially became the brand we know today in 1950, growing and expanding globally through innovation, acquisitions, and partnerships. In the 2000s, it brought trusted brands KitchenAid, Amana, JennAir, and Maytag into the fold. By 2005, they were recognized as the world's biggest maker of home appliances.

Enduring companies like Whirlpool have a remarkable ability to innovate by blending the new with the familiar.

CHAPTER FIVE: ETHOS OF EXPANSION

They've expanded across generations by taking calculated risks and embracing change, all while staying rooted in what they know works.

》》》

THE PLAY: *Diversify so that when you take a chance, you're not betting the house on it.*

Safety nets can foster growth and be critical to survival.

From the moment George Vanderbilt purchased his 125,000 acres in Asheville, North Carolina, he and his successors worked tirelessly to make the estate self-sufficient—an essential part of George's original mission.

Progress came slowly. In 1968, after years of operating at a loss, the mansion finally turned its first profit—$16.24. Today, Biltmore is one of the largest employers in western North Carolina.

With increased revenue comes increased tax, and Ryan Cecil's grandfather, William, was faced with a property tax issue that threatened financial ruin for the family. And so, William expanded the portfolio by developing the Biltmore winery mentioned earlier in the book.

"It became part of the estate planning," says grandson Ryan. "A profitable winery's cash flow could be used to help pay the estate taxes on Biltmore. We could diversify our revenue beyond just tickets."

William borrowed heavily to start the winery, planting the first grapevine in the early 1970s. His risk paid off. Today, the winery produces close to two million bottles of wine per year. "It's really grown into a significant business for us," says Ryan's cousin Chase. "And it's the most-visited winery in the nation, which we're very proud of, considering most wine tourism is on the West Coast."

Biltmore's strategy underscores a powerful lesson in resilience and foresight. Thoughtful planning and adaptability can turn potential setbacks into opportunities for profitable growth and stability.

You will experience setbacks in your growth strategy. Centurions plan for them and confront new challenges promptly. Diversifying your offerings is key.

» » »

THE PLAY: *Don't wait for technology to tell you what's next.*

Technology—particularly AI—is without a doubt the frontier of the future. Centurion companies who do not embrace it risk going out of business

My brother Doug loves writing toasts for family events in the style of a Gilbert & Sullivan song. He's brilliant at it. When I want to toast them, I've historically gone to Doug and asked him to write one for me. But as I learned more and more about Chat GPT, I decided to task it, rather than my brother, with helping me. The first toast was okay, and with more training the toasts became pretty good. The more I trained it, the better it got.

I'm a big, big fan of AI. I have a lot of fun with it and believe it has a great deal of potential. Leaders of all businesses need to continuously study what its impact will be and respond accordingly.

CHAPTER FIVE: ETHOS OF EXPANSION

AI is going to be a threat to some businesses, or, in most cases, an enabling technology that allows them to accelerate their productivity, growth, and innovation.

At Cresset, as we integrate AI into our wealth management and family office organization, one thing is clear: We are embarking on a collective journey. Our goal is to equip advisors as strategic partners, operating as quarterbacks in guiding CEO Founders while adapting to how financial planning, wealth advisory, and family office services will evolve. AI will revolutionize the way we go about our day-to-day business, but it will not change the trust, intelligence, and wise counsel that our clients count on. I expect this change to occur as Hemingway wrote in the novel *The Sun Also Rises,* "gradually and then suddenly." [21]

While AI will undoubtedly transform many aspects of investment management, there are crucial elements outside of portfolios that it will enhance but not replace—our educational programs, peer-to-peer learning and community, estate planning, and coaching CEO Founders and their families with everything from business transition or exit, family office administration, preparing their next generation, and living their best lives.

On a founder's call with a successful entrepreneur and his wife in Chicago, she succinctly and powerfully captured our approach with one phrase: "Life optimized, wealth optimized." I've used this ever since.

As AI becomes an integral part of our business landscape, it will enhance and transform our operations. Those who master its potential will reap significant

---
[21] (New York: Charles Scribner's Sons, 1954), Chapter 13, Page 136.

benefits, profoundly impacting how we leverage technology to optimize both life and wealth. Take mentorship as an example.

When I was in my early twenties and just starting companies, there was no digital world. But I came up with a concept for what I would call a virtual advisory board. My "advisors" included Warren Buffett, Bill Gates, Richard Rainwater, and even Benjamin Franklin.

So if I was starting a business and an issue arose, I would call a meeting—in my mind, of course—of my advisory board. I'd use my imagination to determine what these captains of industry and deep thinkers would do with a particular problem.

What would Warren Buffett say about this? Ben Franklin? It was a wonderful methodology but required reading up on these people. If you didn't know enough about them, how could you project what they might say?

Today, that's doable without all the legwork. Generative AI has allowed me to create a real-time virtual advisory board for myself. I can put anyone on the virtual advisory board, and I have noticed that the answers get better over time as the model gains knowledge and experience from the questions I ask.

There was a time when we'd tell people we were coaching, "You need a mentor. Here's how you go about getting one. It's not easy because it requires a real commitment on the mentor's part to be focused on you, and it's your commitment to follow the advice. But when you do find a mentor, it's magical." Now with generative AI, even someone in the most difficult of circumstances, with the least connectivity, can create an advisory board that will answer their exact questions. Those queries can range from a young person's *Where should I go to college?* to a CEO's *What are the risks I should consider in this proposed acquisition?* or *What's the one thing I could do right now that would accelerate my company's growth?*

Your virtual advisory board will continuously get smarter as you ask better and more thoughtful questions. You can add or remove advisory board members over time, depending on your goals. Maybe you have Steve Jobs on your board, but his answers are too mercurial, or you have Warren Buffett, whose answers may no longer fit where you are with your business—so you switch one of them out, and suddenly you have a different perspective. Recently, I even created a virtual executive coach. I started with Bill Campbell, the legendary Silicon Valley coach from the book *Trillion Dollar Coach: The Leadership Playbook of Silicon Valley's Bill Campbell*. Think of the power for the next generation having access to mentors, advisors, and coaches that were unattainable until now.

AI can reduce friction and frustration, and it raises accessibility, leveling the playing field in areas where disparities once existed and opening opportunities to participate. That said, much like its human counterpart, an AI mentor does not have 100 percent accuracy. Consider it another tool helping you toward your goals, but no toolbox is complete with one singular tool.

Embrace AI, experiment with it, understand its limitations, use it responsibly, and be part of the evolution.

»»»

Cheryl McKissack Daniel understands both the threats and opportunities that accompany a rapidly changing digital environment.

"I like technology," says Cheryl, President and CEO of McKissack & McKissack. "If we can streamline anything and have it completed by some program out there, I prefer that, because humans really need to focus on being creative."

But with so much conversation around AI imposing a danger to the arts, she also knows how concerning the rise of these technologies can be to her designers.

"The contractor could go on Chat GPT and say, 'Give me some architectural designs,' and then I go build it, right? But then, what happens to the architects?"

I imagine those architects will find themselves in new roles, supported by AI, tech enhancements, and robotic assists. There will be amazing tools that provide a way of making humans so much more efficient and effective.

However, I still believe even the most advanced technology cannot fully replace the artistic human.

Years ago I was part of a group that owned a company called Omega, the last remaining manufacturer of photographic enlargers and darkroom chemistry. We acquired the company around 1990, just as the digital age began to take hold and predictions of the end of darkroom photography were widespread.

But as digital technology replaced film and revolutionized commercial and consumer photography, making it more accessible and affordable, the darkroom found a new life as a space for artists. It became the bastion of the artist who valued the tactile, analog process. There were artists who kept the old technology alive for decades while a new generation embraced the digital tools and created new forms of art.

Throughout the history of innovation, we have seen traditional jobs that are replaced due to automation and digital solutions. However, there have always been opportunities for new roles and specialized training, such as in engineering and advanced robotics. And although the number of jobs in certain fields may decline, new higher value jobs emerge, and even entirely new industries.

Technological advancements drive significant change, testing the adaptability and resilience of long-standing businesses. Those that navigate these shifts with agility and embrace the opportunities presented will find ways to thrive and grow.

CHAPTER SIX

BEYOND BRAND AFFINITY

»»»

THE PLAY: *Build the house you dream of living in.*

Imagine your brand is a house. What goes inside to make it attractive, authentic, and a home?

As Avy Stein and I prepared for the launch of our new company in 2007, we came up with scores of names for the business. We liked none of them. So we hired a specialist: a naming company called A Hundred Monkeys, which based its name on the completely random, spontaneous process most people use to name new companies and products, similar to just giving the important task to "one hundred monkeys." We could relate to that.

They came up with ten names, and we picked Cresset, which is the word for the bowl that holds fire at the top of a torch, like the Olympic torch. If you're looking at the torch and its flame from above, that's our logo.

The act of choosing our name really marked the start of our company and our brand. Seven years later, with 500 team members and twenty-two offices, I can reflect on that moment with a unique artifact left behind from early days of ideation. It's what we call our culture card—a standard-size note card with key elements of the company's culture written on it.

While Avy and I strategized and built out our prospective client roster, we paid close attention to the brand we were creating, what it represented, and how it was going to come to life. In that process, we consulted with an expert advertiser, Laura Desmond, an expert in business strategy and marketing, who would help us develop a series of tools to help make sure everyone in the company was on the same page to develop great culture. She led us through her framework and unique methodology to create a living, breathing source of truth for how Cresset, the brand, promised to do business with our customers.

It was just that, a promise. Our culture card (see page 89) might best represent how the brand came to be and how we conduct ourselves. I always carry it with me and at the bottom of the card it reads, "we're building the house we want to live in."

When I think of "building a house," it reminds me of the term often used in high-end fashion: *House* of Couture and the *House* of Ferragamo. These aren't just brands, they're institutions, built on a foundation of craftsmanship, legacy, and a commitment to excellence that spans generations.

We also hear it in sports: "protect the house," which ties into the metaphor of a home. The warmth, the thriving, the growth, and the prosperity within the home resonate

Our Commitment to Lead with Culture

VISION:
To reinvent the way people experience wealth and enhance their financial well-being, by expanding access to a proven ecosystem of ideas, solutions, and talent, because our clients deserve better.

SPIRIT:
Investing the Way It Should Be

VALUES:
We Believe in Great People
Results Focused
Optimistic Energy
Continuous Curiosity
Thoughtful Efficiency
Faster Innovation
Be Direct with Respect
Speed & Responsiveness

ACTION:
Uncompromising Alignment

BEHAVIORS:
Client First
Act Like an Owner
Extreme Accountability
Growth Mindset
Confidence to Question Conventional Thinking
Transparency
Cultivate Diversity
Give Back

We're building the house we want to live in.

deeply. Personalizing a business by thinking of it as a home where everyone is aligned and flourishing can truly transform a business.

Before Avy and I started Cresset, I had never worked with a business where anyone wrote down our culture and identity before launch. Never. We wrote business plans, strategies, tactical papers, white papers. We *talked* a lot about culture and the kind of company we were building. But writing it down for Cresset built the blueprint for not only the house we wanted to live in but for the home into which we would welcome our customers for the next century and beyond. What would our home feel like for them, and what was the meaning inside of it? Those are the questions we set out to answer.

It is essential to take the time to make the essence and mechanics of your brand authentic. This goes well beyond picking a name and a logo and declaring: *I'm in business!*

You need to spend time on the architecture, defining the framework and building blocks of your culture and identity. Then you have to live it, consistently and authentically setting the example, and then repeat and remind everyone about it at every opportunity. Avy and I added our contact information and a place for taking notes on the back of the culture card. We use them as oversized business cards, passing them out every chance we get.

We will often pull our culture card out of our pockets when we're with a client, a prospective team member, or a prospective client. They'll put on their glasses and read the whole thing. It differentiates us, and I believe it's made a difference in our standing in the competitive world. People remember Cresset, our culture, people, and brand.

CHAPTER SIX: BEYOND BRAND AFFINITY

Our biggest competitors were interviewed in a once-every-five-year study on wealth managers and multi-family office management by the Family Wealth Alliance. Those included were major players like Goldman Sachs, UBS, Morgan Stanley, and JP Morgan. When asked to rank their top competitors, Cresset landed at number five in wealth management and number five in family office services. I couldn't believe it. After only six or seven years in operation, that was a remarkable ranking to me.

Surely the giants of our industry weren't rooting for us to be successful, but that we've been identified as the fifth-biggest brand in seven years hasn't gone unnoticed. I credit a lot of that to the special culture and team of employee owners who built a brand that resonated with prospective clients.

》 》 》

The lore of how Jeff Bezos conducts business is legendary. One story from his Amazon days involves the notable metaphor about the "empty chair." Bezos always insisted that an empty chair be left at the meeting table to represent the customer, reminding everyone that they are the most important person in the room. "Obsessing over customer experience is the only long-term defensible competitive advantage," Bezos has said.

Centurion businesses would probably add a second chair—one for the customer and one for the brand. The customer is paramount, but their connection to the brand, and how that makes them feel, is essential to long-term success.

I felt that customer centricity with Ryan and Chase, fifth-generation descendants of George Vanderbilt, in how they talk about their Biltmore Estate as if it's another member of their family.

The name Biltmore was derived from *Bildt*, a Dutch town with citizens of Vanderbilt ancestry, and *more*, an Old English term referring to rolling, mountainous countryside. Yet when you visit the property, it's not just a magnificent rolling, mountainous countryside estate. Every interaction with the people there, from the hotel and restaurant staff to the curators and docents, radiates warmth, accommodation, and genuine engagement. It's evident that the employees carry a deep sense of pride in what they do and loyalty to the brand. Their tenure and commitment reflect the core values of what it means to create an emotional connection with customers and with each other.

Transforming a company name into a brand requires clear identity, consistent experiences, engagement, and strategic cultivation of advocacy. It is the sum of the perceptions, emotions, and experiences associated with a company which, for Biltmore, has developed in the 130 years since George Vanderbilt landed on the name.

Biltmore represents so much: the imagery and the experiences it provides, the businesses it created to make the estate profitable, and the care provided for employees. It's generations of leaders and their stewardship of their home and property, packed with all of that meaning.

"Meaning" may not be a line item on the balance sheet, yet it's where so much of the value in a business lies. Infusing a brand with meaning is what makes the house a home.

CHAPTER SIX: BEYOND BRAND AFFINITY

»»»

THE PLAY: *Harness the emotional connections between you and your customers so they remain loyal.*

Brand affinity is one of the most coveted value propositions in business today. Centurions have spent generations cultivating and respecting the sanctity of that bond.

For Centurion companies, part of brand magic is the shared history felt within the business and by those who continue to embrace it. Newer enterprises have the chance to craft their story and forge exciting bonds with fresh audiences. That connection becomes part of the company currency.

Take a moment to think of an iconic brand—any one that comes to mind. It could be something you use every day, a product or service you saw on TV, or maybe it's something you remember from your childhood. What stands out? Are there any specific colors or shapes that you can see? Maybe a slogan or tagline? A thirty-year-old theme song you still can sing on cue?

Consider how it makes you feel. What emotions do you associate with that brand—happiness, reliability, excitement, luxury? What would your life look like without this brand? How significant is it in your daily life?

This simple exercise demonstrates the remarkable power of branding. The fact that you could instantly visualize a brand accompanied by a wave of emotions and even memories exemplifies how deeply brands are embedded in our lives. This is the essence of brand affinity. It's not just about recognition but also connection, trust, and emotion.

Marketplace trends suggest that today's consumers want products that are local, are made by real people, and invoke nostalgia. In a rapidly changing world fueled by technological innovations, globalization, and digitization, more and more people feel disconnected from their emotional moorings. Buying products that make us feel connected to a place, people, or our past makes us feel grounded. Company builders can tap into these emotions to connect in a powerful way ... for the long term.[22]

Juan Moreno, President of Spanish torta company Inés Rosales, talked to me about this approach. "The legend of our products and brands was built around feelings of happiness," he says. "It's about more than pricing, quality, and shelf life, but also because our products are consumed during milestones or highlights or, in general, happy moments of people's everyday lives."

Lucía Conejo-Mir, Vice President of North American Sales, adds, "It also helps that the company and brand is the name of a real person. Our consumers feel like Inés herself is still there making the tortas. We have a very loyal base; they're not attached to trends or promotions. They're attached to our story."

Since its 1910 founding in Seville, the company continues to preserve the Inés Rosales traditions, which they say

---

[22] "Americans Willing to Spend an Extra $2K This Year to Strengthen Their Main Street," Faire, May 15, 2024, https://news.faire.com/2024/05/15/americans-willing-to-spend-an-extra-2k-to-strengthen-their-main-street; Joan Verdon, "Retro Rewards: How Businesses Are Monetizing the Nostalgia Trend to Win Over New Customers," CO, November 8, 2023, https://www.uschamber.com/co/good-company/launch-pad/businesses-use-nostalgia-for-growth#:~:text=Retro%20Rewards:%20How%20Businesses%20Are%20Monetizing%20the,consumers%20new%20ways%20to%20experience%20the%20past.

CHAPTER SIX: BEYOND BRAND AFFINITY

classifies them as truly artisan, a point they doubled down on repeatedly in our conversation. The unique packaging—once briefly abandoned to cut costs—was quickly restored when customers felt betrayed. And the ill-conceived idea to use cheaper oils was hastily discarded in the name of preserving quality. These decisions extended far beyond mere product and profit.

When customers feel an emotional connection to a brand, it propagates loyalty in the face of competition. "Our consumers have the name Inés Rosales associated with experiences in their everyday lives," Lucía says, recalling her own childhood experience. "I'm Spanish and I grew up eating tortas. One of the clearest memories I have is of my grandmother and me eating Inés Rosales tortas as a snack every afternoon after school."

"This story is not just my story," she adds. "People who consume our products will tell you similar things. Our consumers have very positive memories attached to it. This is why they choose us."

As the company reins were passed down among generations, Lucía says, "We could have feared that the product wouldn't have the same amount of recognition. But even now, the brand has still managed to infiltrate lives."

Juan adds, "All of this has happened very organically. The product hasn't changed in all these years. If anything, we've improved it, and that helps us maintain that connection with the consumer. It's almost like we've never broken that unofficial agreement with Inés Rosales that we were never going to change her essence. There is still an emotional value that continues to be attached to our brand."

Emotional connections yield higher customer loyalty, increased brand engagement, and greater lifetime value. And when consumers forge a strong emotional bond with a brand, they become more than just customers—they become advocates. Research consistently shows that emotionally connected customers are far more likely to make repeat purchases, recommend the brand to friends and family, and remain loyal even amidst fierce competition.[23]

》》》

Fifteen years before Inés Rosales started her business, William Harley, a fifteen-year-old factory worker in Milwaukee, Wisconsin, developed a passion for bicycles. At the time, interest in them had exploded across Europe and America. While working as a draftsman for a company called Barth Manufacturing, William met a young patternmaker named Arthur Davidson. The two bonded over their newfound fascination with machines and engineering; soon they began experimenting with attaching a motor to a bicycle. They were convinced they could create a better-mechanized bike with a smoother, faster ride.

With Arthur's two brothers, William, a toolroom foreman, and Walter, a machinist for the railroad, Harley and Davidson set out to pioneer a new industry, motorcycles.

In 1903, The Harley-Davidson Motor Company started in a shed in the Davidson family backyard. By 1909, the company built a factory that was selling a thousand bikes a year.

---

[23] "Emotional Attachment and Profitable Customer Relationships," Ipsos, February 7, 2017, https://www.ipsos.com/en/emotional-attachment-and-profitable-customer-relationships?utm_source=chatgpt.com.

Harley returned to school for a degree in mechanical engineering at the University of Wisconsin—all part of a quest to become what historians have called a relentless perfectionist, with a single-minded focus of improving his invention.

Today, the iconic bar and shield logo is one of the most recognized logos in the world and for Harley lovers, represents a community, a culture, connected by more than just a love of motorcycles, but to the feeling of freedom, an open road and people just like them, doing what they love. As of this writing, there are more than 1,400 official Harley Owners Group chapters in one hundred countries, offering a shared sense of adventure and collective enthusiasm, meticulously cultivated by the brand.

Harley-Davidson set the standard for infusing heritage and storytelling into a brand. When you do it right, a name and a logo become an ethos of what the brand embodies.

I bet if you were to make a list of the ten most powerful and influential frameworks for shaping a business, alignment of company and customer interests would be among them. When the interests are aligned, great things can happen.

» » »

THE PLAY: *Engage and nurture your community through cultivated and intentional experiences.*

A strong community is a building block for success in life and business.

Good customer experiences lead to an engaged community, and an engaged community can bolster a brand's longevity and relevance in the market. For retailers like Italian fashion brand Isaia, cultivating a retail experience that feels elevated and connective goes hand in hand with selling clothing.

Isaia has long valued the concept of customer experiences in their stores to foster and grow a dedicated following. When my wife Jill and I visited their Capri, Italy, location, we were fascinated by the environment. I could see myself hanging out there, having a meal or meeting friends for a cocktail. Not the usual activities that usually come along with shopping for a suit. But it's Isaia's long-standing approach to creating unique store experiences.

"Several competitors are now building their new stores with a bar inside, something we did fifteen, twenty years ago. Now I'll have to find something else," third-generation CEO Gianluca Isaia tells me.

The connective tissue built into their traditional retail environment distinguishes the brand. Today, major brands will spend anywhere from $500,000 to $10 million-plus annually to build their communities.[24]

The long game, however, is to bring like-minded customers together around products, culture, and experiences. And in today's metaverse, communities of superfans can emerge and follow and connect with their fellow customers across geographic locations, even if they never leave home.

---

[24] Tori Utley, "Facebook Launches $10 Million Initiative for Community Leaders—5 Things You Need to Know," *Forbes*, February 16, 2018, https://www.forbes.com/sites/toriutley/2018/02/16/facebook-launches-10-million-initiative-for-community-leaders-5-things-you-need-to-know; ACCESS Newswire, "T-Mobile Empowers 250 Communities Nationwide with $11 Million in Hometown Grants," news release, December 18, 2023, https://www.accessnewswire.com/818064/t-mobile-empowers-250-communities-nationwide-with-11-million-in-hometown-grants?utm_source=chatgpt.com.

CHAPTER SIX: BEYOND BRAND AFFINITY

»»»

Dungeons & Dragons has reigned supreme in the role-playing, tabletop-gaming space for decades, celebrating its fiftieth birthday in 2024. Today, an estimated fifty million people have "interacted" with D&D since its inception.

Chris Cocks was the CEO of Wizards of the Coast, the publisher of Dungeons & Dragons, three years before Hasbro purchased it in 1999 for $325 million. Chris is now the CEO of Hasbro. "Coming from Wizards," he tells me, "I have this very deep appreciation for superfans and their community. Other brands will say they've got super hardcore fans. And I know they do, but Wizards and the world of Dungeons & Dragons is tip-of-the-spear hardcore fans. And so, they help us. They push the rest of the company to understand the value of community and adopt it in a more visceral and faster way—and not just give lip service to it."

Even Chris's teenage son is engaged. "My son is a big Dungeons & Dragons fan and has a sense of ownership with the game. You can tell by how he talks about it—like it's part of his community, part of his friends' community. The brand built around the game engenders a very passionate group of consumers and participants.

"Having exposure to a bunch of different play patterns and all kinds of consumers, it helps to strengthen the whole," Chris says. "I think that helped us think more expansively about how to engage digitally with fans, how to think about social media, how to think about selling directly to consumers, than if we had been just a toy company bound by constraints and being nervous and defensive about it."

All of this relates to Chris's belief that a diversified portfolio and array of consumers keep Hasbro from stagnating into a staid toy company.

Dungeons & Dragons has weathered dramatic ebbs and flows in visibility and popularity since its invention in 1974 by E. Gary Gygax, a self-described nerd and devotee of J. R. R. Tolkien novels. Gygax sought to combine his love of role-playing games with more conventional board-and-dice approaches. Initially, D&D enjoyed growth in relative obscurity, went underground in the 1980s amid fears that it was rooted in the occult, and rebounded with the perception that it was for anyone not in the "in" crowd, only to make a huge leap in mainstream recognition fueled by the internet and a pandemic that confined us to our homes, looking for things to do.

"Take a look behind me," Chris says on our video call. "I'm sitting in a room with probably twenty-five thousand dollars' worth of D&D stuff, of which Hasbro has probably gotten paid only a thousand. It's a perfect example of cocreation and building a fan-generated economy around a product and around a brand."

Their numbers are staggering.

"I'm gonna give you rough and tough numbers, but we make one hundred fifty million to two hundred million a year on D&D—it probably generates sales in excess of two billion per year. And that's because there's this huge marketplace of miniatures and fan-made toys and adventures and streaming the series and all this other stuff. There's real ownership from the fans who drive that." It's like a D&D economy built by and for the community.

CHAPTER SIX: BEYOND BRAND AFFINITY

Going beyond your brand means that your community sees themselves in what you're building. The moment they feel a sense of identity and ownership, while engaging with your product and other users, they are growing a like-minded community within the home you've created for them. If the foundations are strong, your house will live on.

CHAPTER SEVEN
SUPER STEWARDS

»»»

THE PLAY: *Protect your legacy.*

Be strong stewards of every aspect of your business to preserve it for generations.

Ryan Cecil felt so strongly about stewardship and its application to his business philosophy that he looked into the word's etymology.

"The origin of *steward* is late Middle English, sixteenth century, and it meant a *hall warden*. Initially, that didn't quite resonate with me until you realize that a hall at that time was an agrarian manor home on an estate," says Ryan, great-great-grandson of George Vanderbilt, the man who purchased the land that encompasses the Biltmore mansion.

"So, Biltmore House would have been considered a great hall at that time," Ryan explains. "And the steward's job description was someone entrusted with the care of property, place, people, and the resources necessary to enable that care. I thought this perfectly captures what we do today.

"We're not stewards of just the property and the art collection, the house and stables, but stewards of our legacy of gracious hospitality, stewards of our community, our environment, this wonderful oasis that draws people to Asheville, and, of course, stewards of our financial resources that help us enable it."

The impetus for George Vanderbilt purchasing the land and building Biltmore House was to create a lasting home that embodied his vision for beauty, preservation, and self-sufficiency. His estate exemplified the principles of stewardship and sustainability. At its peak, the property encompassed approximately 125,000 acres, and his decision to sell a portion of that land to the federal government laid the groundwork for Pisgah National Forest, one of the first national forests east of the Mississippi. It was George's wife, Edith, who ultimately completed the sale following George's untimely death in 1914. George and Edith both had a profound commitment to environmental preservation and responsible land management that permeates the culture of the family business legacy today.

Cousins Ryan Cecil, Aubrey Cecil Baliles, and Chase Pickering, along with their entire family, are dedicated to preserving the natural heritage of the cultural destination while adapting to modern needs, ensuring that the estate's legacy endures for future generations.

As Chase put it, "I'm really proud that we've selected that word—*stewardship*—as a core value because it so well represents what we do. I wanted to join the family business because of this whole idea of stewardship. For me, the personal value is nature conservation and how we protect nature. That is some of the most important work we do at Biltmore: managing the land, engaging in the community, and ensuring that we have a beautiful mountain backdrop for a long, long time."

Descendents of George Vanderbilt were always drawn back to the estate by their sense of stewardship. When grandson William Cecil left his career in banking in 1960, he encountered friend and former colleague David Rockefeller on a flight. Rockefeller asked William why he wanted to run such a white elephant. Undeterred, William forged ahead.

The young Cecil had returned simply to "see what could be done about the old family homestead." At that time, it had a serious financial drain that needed to be subsidized by the profitable dairy farm. The interior of the house had also fallen into disrepair, with no funds available to preserve or restore the mansion. The business, drowning in losses, seemed on the verge of collapsing. The young Cecil may have visited to simply see what could be done and left, confident that he could do something great with it.

"Very minimal" restoration work had been done, grandson Ryan tells me. It had been open to tourism for thirty years, but "it was really just a roadside attraction. There wasn't a lot of energy and effort put into it." It would be eight more years before Biltmore turned its first meager profit.

Against that backdrop, William's brother George didn't share the vision. So, they forged a somewhat sad but amicable agreement to split up the property. Neither side has regrets; most family members still live in Asheville and attend family gatherings, Ryan says.

THE LONG GAME

In this case, the Cecil family came to a good solution. It was a fork in the road: two different visions. But such a philosophical rift, which might have ripped some families apart, provides Ryan with an invaluable lesson.

"Particularly for family businesses, to be a type of Centurion business, you have to embrace that stewardship role because that's something you'll have to continue for generations."

Being a steward of your business requires an agreement amongst the family and employees helping to preserve its legacy. It's a collective and deeply held understanding that the enterprise is greater than any one individual.

》》》

By prioritizing the company's well-being over personal ambitions, Hasbro's leadership has consistently demonstrated a shared commitment to preserving its legacy through innovative products. From selling textile remnants and pencils in the 1900s to acquiring iconic toys and games like Mr. Potato Head and Monopoly, the company has consistently focused on the future while staying true to its founding principles and unique identity, stewarding through generations.

It's almost like there's something in the DNA of these organizations that makes them survivors. For Hasbro, incorporated in 1923, perseverance provides perspective on what's important.

CEO Chris Cocks notes the longevity and sustainability of the Hasbro empire.

"I think when you have a company that's as old as we are, and you have brands that have been around for as long as we have, there's a collective understanding that it's more than just a brand.

"Monopoly is from the 1930s. Play-Doh is from the 1950s. G.I. Joe is from the 1960s. Transformers is from the 1980s. Furbys from the 1990s," he says. "These are things that we all grew up with, that our kids are growing up with and we want to make sure our great-grandkids are growing up with."

Take Monopoly.

"We take for granted that Monopoly is a game that ninety percent of American adults have played today—and that will be the same in fifty years, and a hundred years from now. And it's because it's a brand that has one hundred percent awareness among adults in the US."

Not only do most households have Monopoly, "Many of those households probably have five or six versions of it," Chris says. "So, you have almost a stubbornness that you know Monopoly is going to persist. You know it's a historical play pattern. And that becomes more of a growth mindset."

Hasbro leaders focus on making their products relevant for the future rather than "something that is a temporary sugar high for the business that will come and go," he elaborates.

And there's nothing wrong with capitalizing on past successes. Transformers, G.I. Joe, and Power Rangers took on new lives in the movies well after the action figures were introduced. In 2024, Hasbro went to the well again, announcing that it was giving its licensees clearance to reissue first-generation Transformer toys in celebration of their fortieth anniversary. The company likewise expanded its Star Wars presence with a new toy line, four-inch-tall action figures in the Epic Hero Series.

The joy of having products with such a lasting impact is that a company respects everything but fears nothing. "We've had a rough patch here or there with Hasbro," Chris tells me. "Honestly, we probably have a down cycle every twenty to twenty-five years. And as long as you trust in the brands, trust in the universality of the play pattern, and correct yourself back to your founding principles, you're gonna get through it."

When you've been around for a long time, history doesn't repeat itself, but it rhymes. If your business survived a recession, for instance, you may face a new economic downturn with more confidence. Or, if you've survived two wars, you may feel like you can survive whatever geopolitical crisis is thrown your way next. That gives you a certain kind of grace under fire, and a sense of belief that a new company, even one with fresher brands, might not have.

Chris's description frames perfectly what I see as a matter of urgency versus importance. Understanding urgency is like dealing with a ringing phone. On the first ring, maybe you continue on with what you're busy doing. On the second ring, you can likely stay focused. But at the third ring, you start to feel agitated. And by the fourth ring, you inevitably say, "I need to pick up this call."

But here's the thing: We don't know who's actually calling. It could be important, but it could also be nothing, a scam or someone cold-calling to sell you something you don't need. The call feels urgent because it's a disruption, but it's not necessarily important. It may be an emergency or nothing at all.

When something happens in your company, it may feel like that ringing phone—you want to react immediately and answer the call. But the key is developing the discernment between what's truly vital and what just gives the appearance of urgency. A strong sense of your company's purpose and connection to the greater good can help bring clarity and stability when weathering any storm.

》》》

THE PLAY: *Act as an "eternal school" to educate your team and inspire them to deliver on your mission.*

Your mission may be critical to what you're building, but the people who become family on your journey must understand and aspire to do whatever it takes to deliver on it.

When Avy Stein and I founded Cresset, we aimed to build a long-term family office and wealth manager for today's generation of founders. We drew inspiration from great wealth management firms like Bessemer and others, which were established by the visionaries of their time. In pursuit of century-long lessons, I reached out to the Pitcairn Company, a family office with deep generational experience.

It is not an idle mission statement when Pitcairn Co. says it treats customers like family: Looking out for family members was the crux of the company's founding one hundred years ago. For a century, Pitcairn has partnered with some of the world's wealthiest families to meet their needs and drive better outcomes—year to year, decade to decade, generation to generation.

It was founded in 1923 as a family office to serve the needs of the Pitcairn family. But Pitcairn's story really began forty years earlier, in 1883, when John Pitcairn founded the Pittsburgh Plate Glass Company. By 1900, PPG produced 65 percent of the nation's high-strength plate glass and had also become the second-largest paint manufacturer in the US. Today they're known as the Fortune 500 company PPG Industries, which built the family fortune.

John's three sons, Raymond, Theo, and Harold, were managing their affairs independently after their father died in 1916. Raymond was an attorney and understood estate law; he implored his siblings to pool their resources, establishing a family business to preserve the wealth of the Pitcairn descendants, whose numbers were growing exponentially.

In 1988, the Pitcairn Company expanded their services and opened their doors to other wealthy families who were in search of adept wealth management. They coined the term *wealth momentum*, which was not directly related to finances but was rather a mission to educate far beyond dollars. The wealth momentum was a promise to educate their clients on all the different aspects of everything from family governance to family charters. These subjects were a crucial part of the foundation from which the Pitcairns had managed their own family wealth; it became a key part of what they wanted to offer to other families.

Today, the Pitcairn Company includes nonfamily leadership, including its recently retired and first female CEO, Leslie Voth, and the man who succeeded her, Andrew

Busser. The company manages family-focused investments valued at more than $9 billion.

I talked to Rick Pitcairn, the firm's Chief Global Strategist, and his cousin Clark, a fourth-generation family member and company Chairman who also serves as a liaison between families and the firm's executive leadership. Sometimes, he says, younger family members haven't been fully versed on the size of their impending inheritance or how to use it. That's where an executive's empathy for a client can come into play.

"Some families don't enroll their children in the wealth education programs Pitcairn offers," Clark says. Accordingly, he can be among the first to fully brief young clients on what's imminent.

"I've had numerous occasions to talk to younger heirs about what he or she was going to inherit," Clark tells me. "And in many cases, I'd talk them into retrusting it for maybe another nine years so they wouldn't suddenly have access to all this money and not know how to handle it."

Some take Clark's advice, some don't. Among those who do, the approaches and outcomes can vary.

"I would encourage them to explore things, maybe start a business but with some rationality. I'd really question them. I'd make them do a business plan with an appropriate level of their investment. You don't want them to risk their whole inheritance."

One client, Clark recalls, had no idea about what he was going to inherit, so when it was time to receive his impending fortune, there was a lot to consider. He was born in Colombia, adopted by his family in the US, and always wanted to know about his birth mother, so he traveled to South America and found her.

"He called me up and said, 'You know, she became an attorney. She was a poor person when she had me, and couldn't afford to raise me.'" His birth mother wanted to buy a building for her law practice, and the young man wanted to help. He asked Clark if that was a good idea. "I was really skeptical of it," Clark recalls.

He suggested that his young client remember his advice about saving some of his monthly inheritance stipend.

"He said, 'Oh, no, I'm not asking for any money from my trust. I've got the money.' I was so relieved. He had been listening to what I was saying and was putting money aside for years. He'd built up a hundred thousand dollars on his own. That made me feel good—to know he had listened to me."

That kind of customer care for all clients is critical because these days, Clark says, "I spend more of my time working with other, outside families who are coming to us than the Pitcairn family, per se."

In managing family wealth for generations, it's crucial to establish a road map for the future, with "appropriate levels of structure and process," Rick Pitcairn says. "Nobody thinks of this when they're in that first generation of wealth creation. It's as though they feel like all those committees and all that structure is sort of onerous. But it actually builds in some longer-term understanding and ability to get to these educational points that Clark talks about."

Establishing structure and guidelines helps ensure "it's just not one family leader calling the shots with the rest of the family feeling outside the loop," Rick says. "Instead, they're all connected to how it all works.

"You should have families exposed to venues requiring structure, quarterly meetings, audit committee meetings, and so forth," Rick explains. "We have all sorts of governance meetings at Pitcairn, and that lends us a sense of stewardship—the people who put those structures in place and believe in leaving something better off than where you found it. I think that that goes a long way."

Clark notes that companies must create shared values and hold strong to them when dealing with clients, family, and outsiders alike. Same for employees. "It's super important to treat your employees with those same values. Build a culture where people feel good about coming to work, where they're respected, where they're treated fairly. Make it a win-win for everybody on all levels. That is the real key to longevity—creating the values for the client, experience, and/or service, and a great culture for the employees. That is what inspires and transcends generations."

Shepherds of these long-standing businesses, like Clark and Rick, understand that it's up to them to pass the torch to the next wave of innovators, sharing their invaluable knowledge and experience. This transfer of wisdom is a testament to a commitment to nurturing the broader entrepreneurial ecosystem.

They preserve their own legacies and actively share their most effective strategies and insights with future generations of entrepreneurs who are beneficiaries of rich legacies. It's akin to passing down a treasure trove of proven practices, offering a road map to success for those who follow.

That's the true embodiment of stewardship.

》》》

As Gianluca Isaia relaxes in his chair from his office in Naples, he speaks with passion about the unique craftsmanship that has sustained his company through the years. He highlights the vital role of stewardship in preserving the art of tailoring through the generations, emphasizing how such dedication is essential for keeping esteemed clothing businesses, like his, afloat.

Unfortunately, he says, some tailors just don't get it.

"I think stewardship is very important," Gianluca tells me. "There are a lot of very good Neapolitan tailors, and tailors in general who are very generous at sharing their craft. But we had two or three in Napoli, geniuses, really, who weren't so generous.

"Unfortunately, they didn't want to pass their knowledge to the next generation. It was stupid, in a way, because in another twenty years, nobody will remember them. When they passed away, they didn't leave anything."

Gianluca says the trade must move beyond such narrow-minded thinking. He tries to instill in his tailors the value of sharing their craft with future generations.

"What I try to say to the tailors is: 'It's important that you give knowledge and skill to your colleague, to your team. Tomorrow, they will remember you as the one who taught you something real good.'

"I feel it is very important to take care of our customers, employees, the brand, and reputation," Gianluca tells me. "It is my job to ensure that we pass all of that forward to the next generation. That is the future of Isaia."

He envisions tailoring skills becoming their proprietary "eternal school. Our master tailors can teach the young people."

There was a time, maybe ten to fifteen years ago, he says, when tailoring was frowned upon as a profession.

Less so today. "Younger generations are thinking again that to be a tailor is an art. We have a lot of younger people interested in the trade now, and also women are becoming tailors more than before."

To ensure the legacy of the Neapolitan sport coat—the distinctive creation born from Neapolitan tailors adapting the warmer British jacket—Isaia recognizes the necessity of transferring these historic skills down through generations.

When asked whether that will always be a fundamental part of the brand, his response is immediate and emphatic. "Yes! One hundred percent!" he declares with conviction. For Isaia, preserving tradition means more than just maintaining the product; it involves deeply instilling their mission in every worker and equipping them with the expertise to uphold it and deliver.

In a democratic and meritocratic society, it is only natural that those who have mastered their craft would seek to uplift their peers, strengthen their industries, and enhance the overall economy. Helping the next generation helps us all.

» » »

THE PLAY: *Identify what stewardship means for you and your business.*

Leverage the responsibility of carrying your company forward to inform your decisions and motivate you when the stakes are high.

Bryan Loane always assumed he'd join the family business, Loane Brothers, the awning, tent, and party rentals company. But today, in his sixties, he sees his time as CEO waning. His children are not clambering to take on the role, leaving him to wonder about succession, especially given the number of longtime employees he oversees.

"I think about it all the time," he says, "but I'm not counting on my children doing it. But who knows? My daughter and I joked that she'd be the first woman to run the business. But she wants to be a librarian right now. So, we'll see how that goes. But my real obligation is to all my employees. I've got people who have been here for generations."

Bryan and I discussed one way to take care of employees: creating an employee stock option plan, a retirement plan that gives workers partial or full ownership of the company. An ESOP is company funded, and shares of its stock often are allocated based on years of service or compensation.

I told Bryan that my dad used the same technique to keep his Santa rental business going when he wanted to step down. After running the Becker Group for fifty-three years without a clear succession plan, he created an ESOP that employees managed for about a decade before they sold the company to a larger one. To the buyer, Santa Claus was just a sideline, but for my dad, Christmas and Santa were everything. So when Santa became just another division of a public company, he was deeply disappointed.

Our family was Jewish, but for all intents and purposes, my dad, Gordon Becker, celebrated Christmas; it was an important family tradition and time of the year. He was just so passionate about Santa Claus and Christmas. And he was proud of setting up the ESOP, which was something only a few companies were doing at the time. People who had worked for the Becker Group for decades suddenly had shares in the business. Many of them didn't fully understand what that meant, so he still had the same responsibility of finding good day-to-day leaders and having the right governance in place.

Dad was happy with the employee-owned ESOP years, and even stuck around for a year after the company was bought out. He was not thrilled with how the new owners ran the company, and he called my brother and me to tell us. "They don't get it. They really are bad Santas; they're just not good at Christmas, and I don't want to work here anymore."

It wasn't that Gordon Becker, the King of Christmas, had stopped loving the holiday. Rather, he came to the realization that the new owners wouldn't carry forward his vision, acting as stewards of his beloved business. Sometimes, despite your best efforts to guide your cherished enterprise into its next chapter, things may not always unfold as planned. Fortunately, some years later, the public company sold the business back to some of the employees.

Bryan Loane tells me he would consider implementing an ESOP to transition Loane Brothers into the hands of its employees. I remark, "You view stewardship as your foremost duty—ensuring that those who have dedicated their lives to your company continue to have meaningful work and a thriving place to contribute."

Bryan nods in agreement, bringing up a concerning trend: Competitors similar to Loane Brothers, after being acquired by private equity firms, often see their identities erased within a year or two. "It's disheartening," he says, "to see these names vanish and become part of larger entities. But that's the reality of the business world."

Think of yourself as a tenacious steward of your business and its employees; it's one of the most vital things you can do to ensure that they carry on successfully long after you're gone.

Imagine you're wearing a Superman cape with a big S for Stewardship. It motivates you, providing additional energy, a greater sense of responsibility, and a stronger commitment to carry things forward when the stakes are high.

CHAPTER EIGHT
ETHICAL SUCCESSION

>> >> >>

THE PLAY: *Build a succession plan.*

Nothing future-proofs a business better than a well-planned transition leadership, ownership, and governance. But it's not for the faint of heart. An ethical transfer must be well planned and executed, with rules in place to safeguard successions across generations.

Roughly one-third of family-owned businesses in the US survive to a second generation. Only about 12 percent make it to the third. The odds against any business lasting more than a hundred years, family run or not, are even slimmer: only 0.5 percent of US businesses make it that far.[25]

Contrast that with Japan, where business longevity through strategic succession offers a shocking comparison.

---

[25] Kristen Taylor-Martin, "Letting Go of the Reins," Family Business Association, March 4, 2022, https://familybusinessassociation.org/article/letting-go-of-the-reins#:~:text=Only%20about%2030%25%20of%20family,by%20the%20Family%20Business%20Institute.

There are so many businesses in Japan that are over a hundred years old—fifty-two thousand as of 2023—that they have a word for it: *shinise*, which translates quite literally to "old shop."

In a country where over 90 percent of businesses remain family owned, Japan could easily write the book on staying power.[26]

So what's their secret?

I have found that Japanese business culture is infused with an overall principle of continuity from day one, instilling a blend of responsibility and foresight that ensures a business is passed down through generations.

Houshi Ryokan, said to be the one of the world's oldest family businesses, is in its forty-sixth generation of leadership.

Founded in 718 AD in the coastal town of Komatsu, Ishikawa, Houshi is a one-hundred-room traditional Japanese inn, or *ryokan*. Legend has it that a Buddhist monk and teacher, Taicho Daishi, climbed Mount Hakusan to meditate. A vision led him to a town with an underground hot spring said to cure the sick. The townspeople helped him unearth the spring, and a Taicho disciple, Houshi Garyo, built a modest sanitarium lodge—a retreat-like facility that became popular in the late nineteenth and early twentieth centuries.

Over time, this humble lodge evolved into a full-fledged hot springs hotel, offering both medicinal care and recreational activities aimed at enhancing physical and mental well-being. Nestled in a serene natural setting, Houshi has

---

[26] "Characteristics of Family Businesses That Hold the Key to Regional Economic Growth," Big Data Analytics, Teikoku Databank, https://www.tdb-en.jp/big_data/1-2.html.

CHAPTER EIGHT: ETHICAL SUCCESSION

become a sanctuary of health and tranquility, reflecting the inn's deep connection to its origins.

Once visited by empresses and celebrities, today the ryokan represents the best of a bygone era and boasts an opportunity for guests to experience treasured Japanese traditions like soaking in a natural hot spring, participating in tea ceremonies, and wearing traditional kimonos. The owner, Houshi Zengoro, believes his family's compassion and attention to detail is what has kept them in business for so many years across so many generations. While that may be true, the hotel would not be one of the oldest in the world without a carefully crafted order of succession.

For more than 1,300 years, male heirs were passed the reins of the hotel, adhering to a strict father-to-son succession model. When there were no male heirs, the common solve was to arrange a marriage of a strong businessman to the owner's daughter. But in 2013, Houshi Ryokan broke with tradition for the first time in over a millennium as Zengoro made the unprecedented decision that his daughter, Hisae, would inherit the inn.

It wasn't the original plan.

Years earlier, Hisae's brother had been deeply involved in the family business and was designated as the next in line to lead. When he fell ill, Hisae stepped up and took over many of his duties. His health took a turn for the worse, and eventually Houshi Zengoro's only son died, leaving the future of the company's leadership uncertain.

With Hisae as his only remaining child, Zengoro set his sights on finding her a suitable husband who, once adopted into the family, could assume leadership of Houshi Ryokan.

Hisae resisted her parents' attempts to find her a spouse who'd be, in essence, a business partner. "I was looking for a partner and was thinking of moving away after I got married," she said in a 2014 documentary shot for *The Atlantic*.[27] "But now my parents introduce me only to men who can be adopted into the Houshi family. What my parents are thinking is not the same as me, so that's also confusing me."

Hisae's parents came to the realization that they would need to break with tradition in order for their family to retain control.

After forty-six generations, Houshi Ryokan made a critical pivot, breathing new opportunity into its succession structure. For a business so deeply rooted in history and tradition, I can only imagine how Zengoro wrestled with the decision to change a 1,300-year protocol, but by making the bold and correct choice, he's positioned the inn for a stronger, more enlightened future.

And what an amazing opportunity for Hisae to set the example for women leaders. As Houshi Zengoro put it, "To make people want to visit us for the next one hundred years—one thousand years, even—we must align with each generation and offer them something attractive as well as something they can benefit from, in accordance with each time."

The transition of leadership to the first female heir after forty-six generations marks a pivotal moment for Houshi—a clear indication of the ryokan's embrace of modern values. This decision represents more than just doing what's right.

---

[27] https://www.theatlantic.com/video/index/387649/this-japanese-inn-has-been-open-for-1300-years/.

CHAPTER EIGHT: ETHICAL SUCCESSION

It's about balancing a rich cultural legacy with contemporary principles, laying the groundwork for future success.

The challenge Zengoro faced in breaking with centuries-old tradition, while seemingly straightforward to some, was undoubtedly a profound one. Yet in choosing progress over convention, he unlocked an extraordinary opportunity for generations to come.

》》》

Leadership is not a position to be held, but a trust to be earned and upheld. Just take a look at Freedman Seating Company.

Craig Freedman, CEO of the family-owned Chicago business, says his father had a highly developed succession plan from the moment Craig joined the company. But there was a problem. There were three family members available to take the reins.

"The same goes for my stepbrothers Dan and Dave. My father recognized that we all have different capabilities, and not everyone can run the business."

Craig went on to tell me that the family went through both counseling and consulting, working with a respected team to help them navigate this complex situation. Today, the business is set up so that either family members or trusted employees can run it. And that is out of necessity.

"For me, there's no clear successor in my kids' generation," Craig explains. "In the fifth generation, there's only one person working in customer service, and he's not on a management track.

"When it comes to passing the business on, it's more important to put it in the best hands for the company rather than keeping it in the family by default. Ideally, the business, the name, and the values live on. But when faced with the choice between what could be a reckless CEO from the family and a great steward from the outside, the decision is easy."

Spending time crafting a well-defined succession plan is not just a formality but a critical component in future-proofing your company, especially in a family business. The traditional path of passing the reins to the next of kin doesn't always align with the needs of a rapidly changing business environment, the social context, sustainability, or other factors.

Mitigate risks associated with leadership transitions by outlining clear guidelines with adaptability at the core. Generational gaps in interest and ability are inevitable; having a framework primed to accommodate various scenarios is key.

》》》

THE PLAY: *Succession is inevitable. Prepare early and know when to get out.*

Succession will happen one way or another— it's simply a matter of time.

By 2020, Cheryl McKissack Daniel already had a year in mind for her retirement as CEO of McKissack & McKissack: 2030. Cheryl started planning her exit early in her tenure.

"I believe a ten-year timeframe is crucial," she says. "Initially, you come to terms with the fact that you won't

CHAPTER EIGHT: ETHICAL SUCCESSION

lead the company forever. Understanding what succession entails is essential—you need to differentiate between managing the business and owning it, which alone takes several years."

A well-documented and communicated plan provides a blueprint for future generations, guiding them in managing their own transitions when the time comes.

"I began contemplating this about four years ago, realizing that succession is inevitable whether I actively prepare for it or not," Cheryl says.

McKissack & McKissack has thrived as a family-owned enterprise since 1905, yet for Cheryl, the emphasis is shifting away from simply preparing the next of kin for the position of CEO. Instead, her focus is on "cultivating a management team capable of sustaining the business with a priority on stability over entrepreneurial drive."

While she remains hopeful that a family member—whether one of her daughters, her husband's children, or even a niece or nephew—might eventually take the helm, that is no longer their primary objective. For Cheryl, ensuring a stable and capable leadership team is the cornerstone of future success, not the family name.

If the younger generations are viable management options for the future, assessing where they stand in terms of management and determining the qualities needed from future leadership are pivotal aspects of this process. "No one person can run an organization of any scale without skill and cooperation from the team. Children considered for ascension to the leadership spot still need to be fully vetted."

And if that doesn't work out, Cheryl still plans to take care of her family in other ways to nurture and honor their legacies. "I'm open to establishing a family office with a competent management team to help manage the growth and distribution of income, as I aim to step back by 2030."

Preparing for succession is critical, and so is knowing when to let go. Cheryl, sixty-three as of this writing, reflected on a conversation she had about running the business that served as an *aha* moment. As she told a coworker, "I just wasn't having fun anymore."

Cheryl confronts her reality every day. She acknowledges the passage of time, how it impacts lives and businesses. Whether it's about getting older or losing interest in leadership roles, she understands that failing to address succession is, in fact, a bad plan. A recipe for failure.

Her pragmatism is evident in her approach, understanding the need to critically evaluate whether a family member is truly capable of taking the reins. The business deserves a competent leader.

Moreover, her willingness to explore the option of a family office with professional management reflects a deep understanding of the importance in maintaining a high-functioning family dynamic, even if the family is no longer directly managing the business. By thoughtfully considering how to structure the income and preserve the family's legacy, Cheryl is forward-thinking.

Willingness to consider different approaches honors the legacy of a family business while also adapting to modern realities.

》》》

Following the death of her husband, Salvatore, Wanda Ferragamo so successfully set up their children for success that it might have had the unintended effect of making things tougher for the generation that followed.

Wanda outlived her legendary shoemaker husband, Salvatore, by thirty-four years; she died at ninety-six in 2018. She spent her time as a widow further enhancing and refining the family business. And though she granted her children considerable autonomy to ready them for leadership, she also maintained a decisive influence over the company's direction, reflecting her strong vision for its future.

"She dedicated her life to the pursuit of what he wanted the brand to become. It was only a women's shoe label when he died," grandson James Ferragamo told *Footwear News* at the time of her death. "There are not many brands that would have been able to progress in such a way."[28]

Wanda and Salvatore created what I call *real alphas* in their kids. Each capable and authoritative in their own right. Early on, Wanda divided the business domains to be run by their six children. As James puts it, "It was like, OK, you go to Europe to run this. You go to Asia to run that. You're America. You're manufacturing—and you're women's wear." They each ultimately had a business to run and they competed, all working hard for the respect of their mother.

But there was a downside, James tells me. With respect and appreciation for his parents' generation, James pointed out a downside: they held onto leadership too long, and by the time they were ready to transition, the next gen had both missed the opportunity to get involved early, and had taken on their own careers. James and his siblings didn't

---

[28] https://wwd.com/footwear-news/shoe-features/james-ferragamo-wanda-grandmother-florence-italy-shoes-advice-1237700474/

get the same early opportunities to make mistakes and learn from them, like their parents. To James, it seemed their prolonged control didn't leave enough room for his generation to learn from his grandmother's genius.

James felt as though his grandmother, Wanda, had instilled a high level of competitiveness and drive into her children, but without a succession education process, so when the time to transition leadership arrived, they weren't ready and really struggled.

The Ferragamo story echoes the experiences of many founders, some whose hesitancy to let go is both public and legendary. But it's not for the good of the company. There is strength in knowing when to let go. You need to pick your timing. If you do it too early, you're putting someone in place who's not ready, and if you wait too long, your successors, if they're talented, will likely have found other interests and may not be available when it happens to be convenient for you. But with the right preparation, the transition becomes all the more rewarding.

>> >> >>

Sometimes, we meet the exception to the rule in which succession is decided on the fly. The Vanderbilt descendants epitomize a wildly divergent approach to leadership transition from previous generations.

As he neared age sixty-five, CEO William Cecil knew retirement was on the horizon—after all, he was incredibly traditional, and that was the expected age to retire. But he hadn't talked much about succession planning, even with his wife.

CHAPTER EIGHT: ETHICAL SUCCESSION

As he approached his beloved Biltmore's one-hundred-year centennial celebration in 1995, at the start of the milestone dinner with hundreds of people attending, he did something unexpected. He grabbed the mic to welcome guests and added a few words at the end.

"All right, well that sums it up, and Bill Cecil, my son, is now going to be CEO of the company," Bill's son, Ryan, recalls him saying. "It was such a mic drop moment for him. He never came back into the office after that. My dad was only thirty-five."

"When I heard this story as a kid, I remember thinking, *That's great! You're in charge, awesome!*" Ryan says. But Bill quickly brought his son back to earth, reminding him that a ton of responsibility came with the unexpected appointment.

"Papa did have a good team of senior executives who my dad was able to work with; that was helpful. But there was no planning. There was definitely room for improvement on how to plan for future leadership transitions,"

"So, that became the impetus behind *That's a great story but let's not do this again*," says Chase, also a grandson of William and son of Dini Pickering, former Chair of Biltmore's board of directors.

William Cecil's hasty announcement left Bill and Dini to spearhead Biltmore's slow but fervent march toward sustainability. The estate had been turning a modest profit, and William's vision of creating a winery as a new attraction to diversify his profit was beginning to take hold.

But, Chase tells me, "It was Bill and Dini who really made that leap for Biltmore becoming an overnight destination. They opened the Inn on Biltmore Estate and then the projects thereafter that invite guests to stay on property."

Bill and Dini also vowed there would be no succession surprises. They created a family council "to really start talking about succession planning and the importance of family unity, how we have a family mission and core values that go alongside the business," Chase says.

Dini especially devoted time to research, attending conferences and meeting consultants on the topics of family councils, wealth preservation, and transitions in company structure.

"Our first family council meeting occurred when Ryan and I were fifteen years old," Chase recalls. "Bill, the youngest in our generation, was eight. So, we literally had Play-Doh on the table as we were talking about things that were important to us as a family.

"We really built from there, beginning conversations around all of the important aspects that you need in place for multigenerational families. It became an important forum built on trust, where we as a family could come together and begin talking about these things that we felt were important for the continuity of our business for generations."

While William Cecil's mic drop moment is an incredible story and turned out to be a success, what we can learn from Bill and Dini's plan for the next generation is that with the right preparation over time, successful succession can and should be accomplished with no surprises.

» » »

THE PLAY: *Create an ethical will.*

This is your insurance policy, in business and life, that enables you to always find your bedrock.

CHAPTER EIGHT: ETHICAL SUCCESSION

In 2007, I wrote the first draft of my "ethical will." It's a very personal document of more than eighteen thousand words that reflects the values, life lessons, and philosophies I want to share about family, relationships, and business.

It was written to my children, and I update it regularly, but I believe it could serve as a model for how future generations of family business owners should conduct themselves. It's like having an insurance policy that pays dividends in the form of reminding you how to face a crisis, and it helps you reconnect with yourself and the things that are most important to you.

In a conversation with Richard Smucker, Chairman Emeritus of the J.M. Smucker Company, he says the ethical will I've drafted for my family resonates with his family's approach.

According to Richard, three things are needed for a business that wants to become a long-term, multigenerational company.

First, project a strong common value system. When the J.M. Smucker Company was incorporated in 1921, Richard recounts, its values might have been faith-based. That's less true today, as cultural or human values play a greater role in a company's philosophy. There is more than one example in the Smucker family history of sacrificing company control for the greater, longer-term good of the family.

Next, create an independent board of directors, not one stocked exclusively with family members. Without that, Richard says, you'll be missing outside perspectives and lacking accountability.

And lastly, find a strong matriarch. This initially catches me off guard and gives me pause, but then he explains that having women in strong roles creates a balanced dynamic. I couldn't agree more.

I routinely recommend to others that they devise an ethical will—a roadmap to which one can always return. I believe most if not all of our Centurion businesses have at least vestiges of an ethical will reflected in their mottos, visions, or mission statements.

The main purpose of composing my ethical will was to reflect on the lessons I've learned. Honestly, I wrote it out of fear that I might die young and my kids would be left with nothing from me to help them grow up. Thankfully, I'm still here, and my kids have turned into fine young adults. But many things I couldn't have imagined, "both terrible and very good," as I told them in the ethical will, did happen. And the insights I developed as I moved through those experiences felt invaluable to pass along.

Cresset and the many other enterprises I've been involved with have taught me how strong business principles are intertwined with life. These principles tell us to:

- **Create a foundation of bedrock.** This has three essential components: your relationships, your reputation, and your values. Even if things become totally unglued in life or business, you can return to your bedrock and rebuild your life. In that process, you know who you can count on.

- **Nice guys finish first.** Nice people are authentic, take a sincere interest in others, and are considerate of them. They give back and create good karma. Yes, it is important to be smart and competitive, but as

CHAPTER EIGHT: ETHICAL SUCCESSION

far as I'm concerned, being nice is the only way to go through life and business.

- **Let people blossom.** One thing I've worked on as a business leader is finding people who are intelligent, motivated, and interested in the company's vision. As an entrepreneur, I've been guilty of micromanaging, which makes things harder because it limits ideas and doesn't allow people to show what they can do. You may recall that many of the Centurion business leaders we've been talking to throughout this book have encouraged their children, their potential successors, to find their passion—even if it's not the company business—and pursue it.

I closed my ethical will with my fervent wishes for my children:

Stick together and look out for each other; show your mother the love and care she has shown you; do what you love to be happier and more successful; spend time with good people as they greatly influence who we are; and help others by being nice, generous, and kind.

Very specific guidelines for my children, yes, but I believe all of these things can be incorporated into—and exemplify—sound business practices.

CHAPTER NINE
RELATIONSHIPS ARE EVERYTHING

》》》

THE PLAY: *Cultivate connections that have the power to shift outcomes.*

The true measure of resilience extends beyond your standards and reputation, centering fundamentally on the strength of your relationships when you need them most.

I learned a lot about the value of relationships from my dad. When I was about fourteen, he took me on my first business trip to Boston. I was dressed in my best polyester suit from the '70s, and I was struck by how my dad interacted with the people we met. The respect and affection they showed him as their supplier was something I'd never seen before. It was as if my dad had another family, and I was amazed by the depth of those connections.

Years later, after my father sold his business and retired, my brother and I were trying to keep him engaged.

One day, he told me that some of his customers from South America were coming to Baltimore to visit him. At eighty-two or eighty-three years old, even though he hadn't been in business for a decade, his customers still wanted to see him.

He took pride in building meaningful relationships. For him, doing business was about more than just buying and selling his services; it was about developing trust and understanding. He would say, "I know them and they know me, and if there's a year when they need something, I'll be able to support them when they need it the most."

My dad took immense pride in everything he did, whether it was personally delivering something for a client or going the extra mile—literally—by flying out and delivering it himself. These acts became legendary within the company. He not only emphasized the importance of relationships but also demonstrated the power of combining relationships with moments of truth. When his customers needed him, he never let them down, always going above and beyond in ways that left a lasting impression.

》》》

Jensen Huang is widely regarded as one of the most successful entrepreneurs of our time. Yet the future of his company, NVIDIA, was far from certain in its early days, long before its meteoric rise to becoming the third-most-valuable company in the world. During a recent commencement speech at National Taiwan University, I listened to Jensen share the remarkable story of how his start-up once teetered on the brink of collapse.

CHAPTER NINE: RELATIONSHIPS ARE EVERYTHING

As he recounted the three critical near failures that almost wiped NVIDIA off the map before it even arrived—making a costly architectural misstep with its first customer, wagering the company's future on CUDA technology, and withdrawing from the Android and mobile phone markets—he revealed the lifeline that saved him: his relationship with Shoichiro Irimajiri, president of Sega and CEO of Sega America. His very first customer, whom he was on the verge of letting down.

When Jensen cofounded NVIDIA in 1993 with his friends Chris Malachowsky and Curtis Priem, the prospect of competing with the world's leading tech giants in the realm of AI wasn't even on his radar. At the time, Malachowsky and Priem were engineers at Sun Microsystems, and Jensen was a director at LSI Logic in San Jose, California. Having recently lost an internal dispute at Sun about the future direction of its technology, Malachowsky and Priem were eager to embark on a new venture. So they met their Silicon Valley buddy with a keen interest in the next wave of accelerated graphics technology at their local Denny's to talk.

When Jensen was profiled in 2017 as *Fortune*'s Businessperson of the Year, he recalled that Denny's meeting. He was just twenty-nine years old.

"We believed this model of computing could solve problems that general-purpose computing fundamentally couldn't," Jensen says. "We also observed that video games were simultaneously one of the most computationally challenging problems and would have incredibly high sales volume. Those two conditions don't happen very often. Video games were our killer app—a flywheel to reach large markets funding huge R&D to solve massive computational problems."

With just $40,000 in the bank, NVIDIA was born.

NVIDIA's first application of an accelerated computing product was their operating chip for 3D graphics for PC gaming. The industry was shifting away from 2D to 3D graphics, so they invented an unconventional 3D approach called forward texture mapping and curves, which was substantially lower cost. It won them a contract with Sega to build their new game console, which would compete with the hugely popular Sony PlayStation. For Huang, this contract was the ticket to funding the company.

After just one year of product development, crisis hit, a *moment of truth*.

Jensen and his team of engineers realized their architecture was fundamentally wrong. If they continued with the project, they would end up with an inferior technology, too outdated to compete. Whether they finished the project or abandoned it, the result would be the same: They would be out of business.

Jensen had one card left. He picked up the phone and called Shoichiro Irimajiri.

An engineer who once designed engines for Grand Prix motorcycles and Formula One race cars, Irimajiri, known in the US as Iri, had taken a liking to Jensen in the development of their project together. He was impressed with the young man's passion and vision.

"I contacted the CEO of Sega and explained that our invention was the wrong approach," Jensen said in his commencement speech at NTU, "that Sega should find another partner, and that we could not complete the contract and the console."

CHAPTER NINE: RELATIONSHIPS ARE EVERYTHING

Jensen went on to explain his embarrassment at asking Iri to still pay out their contract, $5 million—otherwise NVIDIA wouldn't survive. "To his credit and my amazement, he agreed. His understanding and generosity gave us six months to live." What started as a *moment of truth* quickly transformed into a *moment of trust*.

In those six months, NVIDIA developed a breakthrough chip, RIVA 128, and rescued the company, going public two years later. Today, NVIDIA is valued at more than $3.4 trillion.

Jensen is one of those rare cofounders still running his company twenty-four years later. And as he weathers further storms, he has fortified NVIDIA using Centurion principles. By confronting his mistake directly with his customer, with humility and seeking help, he was able to sustain his business from the start—but had it not been for the strength of the relationship he'd cultivated with Iri, you might not be reading this story.

》》》

When I talk to James Ferragamo, he reflects on the company's long-standing partnership with Saks Fifth Avenue, a relationship that began in 1927, nearly one hundred years ago, when Saks started selling Salvatore Ferragamo's shoes. At one point, Saks was Ferragamo's biggest client. Over the years, Saks and Ferragamo have celebrated their collaboration in various ways, including in 1991 when Saks exclusively displayed Ferragamo in their New York City flagship store windows in commemoration of sixty-four years together. The Ferragamo family was on hand to celebrate.

James Ferragamo has worked closely with Saks to continue to nurture the relationship, especially as retail has moved beyond brick-and-mortar stores and adapted to online sales. What strikes me most is how Saks reacted when Ferragamo expanded into direct-to-consumer sales. It could have meant the end. But Saks remained committed to their relationship, especially as the retail landscape began to shift dramatically.

The ties between Ferragamo and Saks go even deeper. Before James Ferragamo joined the family business, he followed the family edict of first gaining experience outside the company. As part of their family constitution for succession planning, this rule ensured that each new generation brought fresh perspectives and independent insights to the legacy of Ferragamo. (The family clearly follows the first play of ethical succession—a well-planned and executed process.)

As James developed his business career, he first spent time at Goldman Sachs to grow his financial knowledge, and then took a job at Saks Fifth Avenue. Years prior, as a testament to the relationship, James's uncle Massimo Ferragamo had also worked at Saks, where he was even invited to join their executive training program. Massimo would go on to become Chairman of Ferragamo USA. James was brought in to Saks as a buyer. While there, James says, he focused on learning merchandising, ultimately preparing him as an expert in how to sell to the Saks customer. It's a partnership that makes sense.

The Ferragamo–Saks Fifth Avenue cornerstone relationship is an example of trust. Bringing a client in house to learn the ropes is contingent upon it benefitting both parties, particularly when the client leaves to grow the family

CHAPTER NINE: RELATIONSHIPS ARE EVERYTHING

business. It doesn't always work. But in an industry where competition is fierce and alliances often fragile, making the extraordinary effort to maintain such a relationship demonstrates the importance of collaboration and long-term vision in driving success.

》》》

THE PLAY: *Consistently evaluate your relationships.*

Knowing when to recalibrate can be the key to sustaining the long-term value of your relationship. Recognize when to step back or seek help to preserve and maintain its health.

No matter how much you nurture your relationships, there are times when even the most promising partnerships falter. How do you respond when a relationship starts to go south?

The answer, I believe, involves a three-step process that I've developed over time and included in my ethical will:

1. **Confront your reality every day, be it in life or in business.** With only one life to live, it is critical to face the truth of your circumstances head on, and not just when the going gets tough. Regularly assessing the state of your relationships allows you to identify potential issues before they escalate. Acknowledge when a partnership is no longer serving its intended purpose, and be honest about its impact on your business. Ignoring or delaying this confrontation can lead to greater problems down the road.

2. **What am I tolerating but shouldn't be?** My favorite question. Now that you've confronted your reality, it's time to address it. Maybe you've identified a chronically

bad long-term relationship that's not getting better. Recognize its detriments and consider whether it's possible to salvage it through open communication and adjustments. If not, be prepared to make the difficult decision to part ways.
3. **Make a request or make a plan.** When you are faced with a problematic partnership or crisis, you have two options: Ask for help or mentorship, or, if assistance isn't available, take ownership and devise a plan yourself. Complaining is not an option. Worrying is a terrible use of energy.

The third principle came from a life coach I decided to hire when I turned forty. I had been running my own businesses since I was nineteen, and although I had seen success, I thought it was time to get some outside guidance.

He was from New York and visited once a month. In our first meeting, he said, "If we're going to work together, there are two things you need to understand. First, are you a man of your word?"

"Yes, of course," I responded.

He challenged me, saying, "No, you answered too quickly. I need to know if you're truly a man of your word. If we agree on something and you commit to it, I expect you to follow through. If not, I will terminate our coaching relationship."

I assured him I was committed. Then he laid out the second point: "When faced with a problem or crisis, you have only two productive choices: make a request or make a plan. People often get caught up in worrying or dwelling on the issue, but these are not productive. You can

CHAPTER NINE: RELATIONSHIPS ARE EVERYTHING

either ask for help or create a plan to address the situation yourself."

He explained, "For example, if you're facing a business challenge, you might make a request for assistance, such as asking for help from a consultant or requesting an advance from your bank. Alternatively, if no help is available, you need to make a plan and take action yourself. These are your only real options."

After putting his advice to the test for over two decades, I believe it's accurate, particularly as it applies to relationships. If you've confronted the reality that you're struggling with a partnership, whether it's a vendor, customer, or employee, address what's not working and propose solutions, like seeking external help from a mediator to resolve conflicts or changing the framework of the relationship. And if your efforts don't yield results, then you need to make a plan. This could mean reassessing the relationship's value, establishing new boundaries, or, if necessary, preparing for an exit strategy.

Not long ago, Cheryl McKissack Daniel faced a challenge that boiled down to a relationship problem. Her company, McKissack & McKissack, was the project manager on a revamp of the Central Terminal at New York's LaGuardia Airport. "I had an issue going on there, but before I could address it, I had to figure out, who's really in charge?"

It's a seemingly simple question, but navigating the true sources of power can make all the difference in resolving complex issues.

"Oftentimes, the person who's really in charge is hiding behind a whole bunch of people who act like they're in charge," Cheryl tells me. "That's the strategic part in building relationships. It's finding out who really has power here and then getting to that person."

Once she identified the person in charge, she realized their differences weren't merely a clash of opinions but could instead be attributed to something more fundamental and frankly, manageable.

"He was from Spain," she says. "I soon realized that the language barrier between Spanish speakers and English-speaking Americans goes beyond just accents. It's a clash of two distinct cultures trying to collaborate. Confronting this reality, I'm exploring every possible avenue to overcome the challenge. It's not easy, but I'm committed to working through it.

"There's a way of managing construction projects in our respective countries that are very different. For example, price point of staff is very different. We pay a whole lot more here in America than they do in Spain—that's another negotiating point that I have to deal with a lot."

In confronting her reality about her client, Cheryl can now adeptly navigate the innate complexities of their partnership to enhance the health of their shared endeavor at LaGuardia.

"At the end of the day," she says, "it's sitting down with people and understanding that they're human. They may not look like me, but they are human just like I am human. And we do better by working together as opposed to working against each other."

I find more value in cultivating, maintaining, and building relationships than in terminating them. Before opting to abandon a relationship, it's better to invest in

CHAPTER NINE: RELATIONSHIPS ARE EVERYTHING

understanding and addressing the underlying challenges. A potential setback can be transformed into a powerful, enduring alliance.

That said, there are times when this becomes unproductive. It's important to acknowledge when the other party doesn't value your relationship the way you do. Maybe it's a company or customer taking advantage of you, mistreating your employees, or refusing to allow you to maintain a reasonable margin. In such cases, you might not simply find yourself unhappy with the energy you invest—business models could be jeopardized, and you're probably better off without that company or customer. In that case, a clear, clean, and forthright exit is the best course of action.

In the delicate dance of business relationships, confronting the stark reality of any partnership is not merely an option, it is a prerequisite for success. Only by facing these truths can we repair and rebuild the connections that are vital to our ventures while protecting ourselves from the ones that threaten them.

》》》

THE PLAY: *Cultivate trust and transparency.*

Trust is the bedrock of enduring success, ensuring that there are no surprises or shortcuts between you and your customers.

In the realm of leadership, few concepts hold as much weight as trust. Frances X. Frei, a distinguished professor at Harvard Business School and an expert in leadership and organizational behavior, has dedicated her career to exploring the intricate dynamics of trust and its profound impact on team effectiveness. She believes that trust is not merely a soft skill or an abstract notion; rather, it is the cornerstone upon which empowering leadership is built.

Frei asserts that trust is essential for fostering an environment where individuals feel safe to express their ideas, take risks, and collaborate authentically. She emphasizes that leaders who cultivate trust within their teams create a foundation for innovation and resilience. When team members know their leader has their best interests at heart, they are more likely to engage wholeheartedly in their work and contribute their unique perspectives.

The value of trust cannot be overstated for The Hartford Insurance Group's historic relationship with its clients.

"Trust is massive," says Laura Marzi, Chief Marketing Officer of Employee Benefits. "It ensures that you're going to be transparent. Trust ensures that there aren't 'gotcha' moments in terms of how you present whatever it is you're selling. Trust ensures that you're not going to take shortcuts."

One of the nation's oldest insurance firms, The Hartford has built a reputation for reliability and integrity, fortifying existing partnerships over the years while continuously drawing new opportunities. In keeping trust at the center of their business practices, The Hartford's successfully weathered market upheavals and remained resilient through historical events to transcend centuries.

"That concept of trust might not be the sexiest idea out there, but I'll tell you what: When the market crashed in 2008, we came through it while other companies did not. And we weren't necessarily on a too-big-to-fail list. The trust and support from the brokerages we work with and the customers that we had insured saved us."

CHAPTER NINE: RELATIONSHIPS ARE EVERYTHING

"The idea of trust is not necessarily given the credit that it's due," Laura says. "It's a long-game play. Many insurance companies compete on price or technology, but we've taken a different approach. Our commitment to building and maintaining trust over more than two hundred years reflects our deep understanding of risk management. It shows that we have the right people assessing and managing risk with unwavering integrity and expertise. We take it very seriously."

Laura also tells me that unlike competitors who may prioritize technological advancements or pricing strategies, The Hartford invests strategically in cutting-edge tech while maintaining its focus on foundational principles. Customers and brokers demand honesty, transparency, well-underwritten products, thorough research, and actuarial pricing based on extensive data analysis.

While some of their competitors may tout innovative features like mobile apps and advanced algorithms, Laura explains that these tools are meaningless if the underlying product lacks reliability.

"We are not a company that is experimenting with getting into a business and then maybe quickly exiting because the margins don't work. Not everyone in the industry has the same priorities." In the end, a product's true value is measured by its performance in real-world scenarios and the support provided to customers, not just the bells and whistles of technology.

So, how does a company founded in 1810—trailblazing in fire insurance, pioneering wage and benefit coverage for workers, and underwriting the iconic Hoover Dam—maintain and deepen trust with its customers in today's ever-evolving landscape? It involves doing more than resting on one's two-hundred-year-old laurels.

"It's really easy to go back and look in the rearview mirror and say, 'We have two hundred years of expertise in protecting individuals and families and businesses.' Those are irrefutable truths. But in terms of meeting the needs of the market and continually transforming ourselves, what we've been able to do is inject a lot of humanity into our business." The Harford sets the bar with the number of feedback loops and customer touchpoints. That, along with the industry's largest dataset, is how they provide support in what is often someone's most difficult moment.

Humanity goes beyond meeting business needs. It means understanding the real lives and challenges behind each policy, recognizing that trust isn't just built on numbers or contracts. It's built on empathy, relationships, and the commitment to stand by clients. In a world driven by tech and price wars, it's this human touch that keeps a legacy company relevant and trusted for centuries.

》》》

Bedrock. I've long been drawn to that term. It represents the solid foundation on which we build relationships. In both life and business, during times of great challenge, we search for something solid to rely on. At first, you might encounter things that feel shaky or uncertain. But eventually, as you keep looking, you hit bedrock—the things you can really count on when you need it most.

In 1974, my dad's company reached a critical juncture. His Santa Claus business, being highly seasonal, was

CHAPTER NINE: RELATIONSHIPS ARE EVERYTHING

always vulnerable to downturns. That year, a rough season pushed him to the brink of bankruptcy, where one bad year could have meant the end.

He approached the banks for help, but they turned him down. Out of desperation, my dad turned to his friends, his college buddies, and asked for support. Remarkably, they stepped up and collectively lent him a million dollars to restructure the business. Without that support, the company would have folded.

What struck him the most was that some of the friends who he hadn't even expected to help came forward. It must have been a deeply gratifying moment to realize that the people he'd valued for so many years were the ones who ultimately saved him and his business. My dad often joked that his friends "saved Christmas." Those relationships had become his bedrock.

In life and business, you need something solid to lean on, not something that shifts or crumbles like sand. You want to build on a foundation that's unshakable with trustworthy, loyal relationships you can always count on.

As I reflect on the challenging chapters in both my dad's life and my own, those experiences have solidified my understanding of what "bedrock" truly means. To me, it comes down to three core elements: your reputation, your values, and most importantly, your relationships. You can lose everything else, but if those foundations remain strong, you can always rebuild.

CHAPTER TEN
TIME HORIZONS

»»»

THE PLAY: *Embrace the Centurion's lens.*

Shift your focus from immediate pressures to long-term vision, enabling your business to weather short-term crises while pursuing enduring goals.

In 1980, a bold new experiment in news was launched by media mogul Ted Turner. The Cable News Network, or CNN, became the first twenty-four-hour television news channel. At a time when the news was limited to daily broadcasts and scheduled programming, CNN took a groundbreaking step by offering news coverage around the clock.

For the first time, global audiences could tune in for breaking news coverage in real time. But not without consequence.

With the advent of a twenty-four-hour news cycle, we entered an era in which every problem, crisis, and challenge is magnified on a continuous loop. The barrage of information, coupled with the spread of misinformation, has sparked profound political and social consequences. In today's environment, the long-term vision crucial to businesses enduring is often overshadowed by the lure of short-term gains, tempting leaders to prioritize immediate results over the bigger picture.

Investing in a long-term perspective is more valuable than ever. It helps put what might feel like insurmountable challenges into context. By shifting your focus and trusting in the future, you can navigate crises with greater clarity—what seems catastrophic today often diminishes in significance over time.

Without that broader view, problems that are continuously put in front of us via wall-to-wall news coverage and social media can drain your energy. You end up addressing every minor setback as though it's the end of the world. A long-term mindset helps you see past immediate distractions, offering clarity amid the chaos.

The long-standing companies we've explored in this book have weathered crises like depressions, recessions, world wars, and global pandemics. Their approach transcends mere survival, revealing the essence of the long-game mindset. These leaders invested in the future, minimized distractions, and demonstrated remarkable resilience.

I'm reminded of one of the first business ventures with my brother, Doug. Castle Foods imported gourmet food from Europe and Asia at a time when most Americans consumed diets of meat and potatoes. Castle Foods introduced Americans to artisanal, organic products like Italian olive oil and French preserves.

It was an incredible business, and walking through the warehouse was a sensory experience, with different gourmet treats on every shelf. The man who ran the company, a second-generation leader, taught me an important lesson when we first faced a significant challenge. He came into my office and said, "I just want you to know, it's not as bad as it looks, and it's not as good as it looks."

That comment always stuck with me. It was a call to put everything in perspective. If someone tells you they've landed a major account, sure, that's great, but in the perspective of a one-hundred-to-two-hundred-year business, it's probably not cause for a ticker-tape parade. Similarly, when someone tells you about a loss or a lawsuit, it's unlikely to run the company into the ground. That long-term view builds resilience and allows you to stay grounded.

I remember something that my mom's life partner, Bob Meyerhoff, who has always been a trusted advisor in our family, said to me when I called him to talk about the state of the world, which was riddled with political chaos and uncertainty. I wanted to help make sense of it for my kids.

When I called him, he was nearly a hundred years old. He still had the clarity to say, "Eric, I believe in America. I believe in democracy, entrepreneurship, and capitalism. I lived through World War II, the Great Depression, Vietnam, and more. This is just a moment in time."

His perspective was comforting, and it reminds me of the long-term thinking of these enduring companies. They operate with a belief that the future can and will be better, and that's a powerful way to run a business and live a life.

I find it fascinating to think in terms of one-hundred- or two-hundred-year time horizons. A time horizon is essentially the length of time you plan to hold on to an investment. While a long-term time horizon in the financial world is typically around ten years. I'm talking about planning for a century or more. In a global era dominated by nimble start-ups, reactive planning, and rapid innovation, companies in places like Japan and Europe lead the world with this long-term mentality.

A company's time horizon shapes its approach to risk, innovation, and resilience, balancing short-term pressures with sustained vision. Conventional planning often involves one-, five-, and ten-year models, providing a structure for immediate and medium-term goals, which may fall short for businesses with ambitions that stretch beyond a typical business life cycle.

Yoshinori Hara, dean and professor at Kyoto University's Graduate School of Management, underscores that long-standing firms often emphasize sustainability over immediate profit maximization. Hara, who spent a decade in Silicon Valley, notes that the focus in Japan is on ensuring that businesses are handed down through generations, aiming for long-term viability rather than short-term success.

Moreover, in Japan, closing or selling a company is often seen as a failure, a sentiment deeply ingrained in cultural values, says Michael Cusumano, professor at MIT and former initiative leader at the Tokyo University of Science.[29] This mindset prioritizes continuity and the preservation of existing firms over the creation of new ones.

Unlike the move-fast-and-disrupt-things dynamic of business within the US economy, Japan's commitment to

---

[29] Bryan Lufkin, "Why So Many of the World's Oldest Companies are in Japan," *BBC*, February 12, 2020, https://www.bbc.com/worklife/article/20200211-why-are-so-many-old-companies-in-japan.

maintaining established firms highlights a dedication to long-term stability and intergenerational legacy.

»»»

The Henokiens, a group founded in France in the 1980s, exemplifies what it means to stretch a time horizon as far as the mind can see.

Their name draws inspiration from a biblical figure: Henok (Enoch), who is said to have lived over three hundred years before being taken to heaven without experiencing death, according to some interpretations.

The group was established by Gérard Glotin, a descendant of Marie Brizard, the creator of the anisette liqueur in 1755. Glotin, intrigued by businesses with deep-rooted legacies, embarked on a yearlong search for companies that had endured for at least two hundred years. He identified seventy-four such family-run enterprises and invited around thirty of them to a founding meeting in Bordeaux, France, in 1981.

Today's Henokiens must meet a two-hundred-year longevity requirement, with management or board representation by a descendant of the founder. The Henokiens remain predominantly European, with the highest number of members from France (sixteen), followed by Italy (fourteen), Japan (ten), Germany (four), Switzerland (four), Netherlands (two), Belgium (two), Austria (two), England (one), and Portugal (one).

Membership in the Henokiens Association is determined not by corporate power but by a company's enduring stability. As a result, the association includes a diverse range of businesses, from globally recognized names to less prominent ones, all united by their solid, long-standing foundation.

Despite their family origins rooted in the past, Henokiens are forward-looking. They strive to engage the next generation of leaders by showcasing how their venerable family businesses have perpetually met the challenges of globalization, sustainability, and respect for human values.

In today's fast-moving business world, firms must stay competitive, adapt quickly to change, seize opportunities presented by globalization, and find funding when a crisis hits. Consequently, ownership changes are accelerating, entrepreneurs are selling faster, and second- and third-generation businesses face growing pressures. But because of their collective longevity, Henokiens are an exception to the global economic landscape. Their unique backgrounds share common values that unite them, such as respect for product quality, human relationships, and shared expertise across generations. They reflect enduring strategies that we've seen in this collection of Centurion enterprises: agility, ability to pivot, strong culture, dedication to sustainable innovation, succession planning, and long-term vision.

Only one country not on the European continent has been welcomed into the Henokien fold: Japan.

We can all take a page out of the Japanese and Henokien playbooks. They operate with a long lens, planning not just for the next few decades but for several centuries, demonstrating a profound commitment to sustainability and foresight.

CHAPTER TEN: TIME HORIZONS

》》》

THE PLAY: *Be flexible and adapt for the future.*

A long-term vision requires agility within the framework of a broader, future-focused plan.

I met once with leaders of a Japanese company involved in the earth-extraction industry, essentially mining and energy, that had been around for over three hundred years. During our discussion of a recycling project, they shared their long-term perspective: Extraction won't be sustainable in the next three hundred years due to environmental concerns. As a result, this company was shifting its focus entirely to the circular economy, emphasizing recycling and ecological practices.

It was fascinating to see how they were planning for the next three hundred years, reflecting on their extensive history, confronting reality, and adapting to future needs. Their historical awareness guided their shift to sustainability.

As Kyoto University Dean Yoshinori Hara suggested, the strategy of prioritizing long-term viability over short-term gains is a common theme among the companies profiled in this playbook. When it comes to sustainability, Biltmore Estate exemplifies a commitment to that mindset, emphasizing environmental stewardship to ensure its legacy endures for generations to come.

Ryan Cecil credits his father, Bill, for his meticulous attention to detail. "He notices even the slightest misalignment, like slanted signs, during our property walks." Bill shares the long eye with Massimo Ferragamo!

His aunt, Dini Pickering, has also always pushed for a strategic, future-oriented approach, creating a strong team and family dynamic: Bill leads the company while Dini oversees the board and family office.

Elaborating on how Biltmore approaches long-term planning, Ryan says, "We consider a five-hundred-year perspective, sometimes joking about what a thousand-year plan may entail. It's this long-term view that helps us as stewards of this estate to sustain the property through various economic cycles."

Even short-term plans focus on long-term gains, Chase adds: "We prioritize preservation with a twenty-year time horizon, conducting comprehensive studies and setting priorities for the next two decades." The family remains agile, adapting to evolving needs and environmental changes.

Rich histories offer a unique approach to time horizons, balancing long-term visions with a disciplined sense of urgency. While long-term visions often unfold nonlinearly, taking incremental steps and learning from successes and failures is key to achieving them.

》》》

Cheryl McKissack Daniel is intrigued by the idea of planning for one hundred years but recognizes the challenge of that given younger generations and shifting trends.

"In Japan, I think they're probably more consistent in their marketplace than we are in the United States," she says. "We don't know what the trends are. Who would have thought we'd be where we are politically today versus ten years ago? You don't even know what tax structure we'll have in ten years."

Cheryl focuses on an audacious ten-year plan for McKissack & McKissack, outlining where they want to be in that timeframe in terms of revenue and other goals.

Craig Freedman from Freedman Seating also shares in Cheryl's apprehension of planning too far into the future.

"We don't plan one hundred years into the future," he explains, "and we're not even focusing on ten years ahead. The rapid pace of technological change has dramatically shifted our time horizons.

"Today, planning for two or three years is considered a long-term outlook. While it's valuable to consider possibilities for the next twenty-five or one hundred years, setting such distant goals for the company isn't practical. We must stay nimble and adaptable, as the rapid evolution of technology makes long-term planning more challenging."

Craig is right about the value of staying nimble. In an era where change is constant, flexibility becomes crucial. While long-term vision is essential, the ability to adapt swiftly to new developments and unforeseen disruptions ensures that a company can remain relevant and resilient. Balancing a clear, strategic outlook with the agility to pivot as needed allows businesses to navigate the complexities of modern markets while still aiming for enduring success.

I've been working diligently with my partner Avy and our team to build a hundred-year business with Cresset. We truly believe that, even in today's landscape of technological disruption, this vision is achievable. The idea is to make embracing digital transformation one of our core principles, navigating technological changes by integrating digital solutions into our operations. Our long-term perspective helps us recognize a common pitfall that many companies face: becoming too comfortable with a successful business model, product, or service, and failing to identify emerging threats until it's too late.

It's like a fly buzzing around an elephant, an annoyance that is initially easy to overlook. Most companies don't recognize the emerging threat early enough, and suddenly the fly grows into something bigger and more formidable. And then, they get stung.

The beauty of adopting a hundred-year horizon is that it encourages leaders to understand that even our strongest current offerings won't remain so indefinitely. Over the course of a century, products will evolve multiple times. Therefore, it's crucial to ensure that our core values, business culture, and commitment to innovation remain constant, allowing us to adapt and reinvent ourselves as necessary.

» » »

THE PLAY: *Build a mission with a business, not just a business with a mission.*

A long-term commitment to purpose is essential for enduring success. Prioritize your mission to drive action and allow profit to follow.

I was dying to meet legendary business leader Mats Lederhausen after reading about him in *Enlightenment Magazine* in 2005. A visionary leader renowned for his profound insights into mission-driven business strategies and sustainable growth, Mats transformed organizations and fostered their long-term success.

I wanted to know his thoughts on what leadership role corporations should take in improving the environment.

When I called his office, I told his assistant I was calling from a private equity firm. She turned me down. But when Mats learned about my interest in education, he took my call. That began a long and deep friendship of almost two decades. Not only was Mats one of the first members of Cresset's advisory board, he is also part of my bedrock.

An influential thought leader, Mats exemplifies the power of prioritizing quality over short-term gains by aligning business practices with core values to build resilient, purpose-driven enterprises. I spoke with him to gain his perspective on future planning for modern businesses while staying true to a mission.

"I believe capitalism would benefit from a more human-centric approach, and society would be better if more companies embraced the commitment of playing the long game," Mats says. "My perspective comes from the belief that I'm not in business merely to make money; I'm in business to inspire human progress."

People often think of business as transactional: the exchange of goods and services for money. Mats values much more than that; it's knowing what your business stands for and what you stand for yourself. His commitment to quality and purpose is central to his long-term perspective.

Mats explains, "There's an old ship maker outside Newport News, Virginia, that has been around for hundreds of years. They have a big rock outside their shipyard with an inscription that reads, *We shall build good ships here; at a profit, if we can; at a loss, if we must; But always good ships.*

"Although making a profit is important for survival, the goal isn't just to make money. The overarching goal should be to create something great, and if profit follows, that's a bonus."

Focus on profit over mission is why so many companies don't last, Mats believes. Embracing a long-term commitment to quality and purpose is essential for perennial success.

Mats now runs his family office with his son, focused on ventures that all have a mission. "Purpose is paramount; it's why having a purpose bigger than just the product matters. Something that defines what you are setting out to achieve and why it matters."

Most family offices focus on the long-term management of a family's wealth. It's not often that they have a mission, governance, or purpose. They don't understand their *why*, and they're not creating their own culture. As a result, they excel in managing investments but fail to adequately support the family. Or, they provide so much support that they diminish the motivation and capability of future generations—family members become so dependent on it that the drive and entrepreneurship that originally created the wealth is sucked right out of them.

Families grow exponentially, and when people don't have their own careers or things to do, the family members can totally dissipate the wealth.

That is the opposite of what we wanted for our families when we started Cresset.

CHAPTER TEN: TIME HORIZONS

Cresset was an amazing opportunity for reinvention. How lucky I was to be able to start something later in my life and say that we were going to build something with no compromises. We could, and did, set a high bar for the people we brought in, and we made them all owners. We wanted to create a great culture, a palpable culture with people who were extremely capable but also kind. This applied to clients, too. They also had to be good people or it wouldn't work.

»»»

As you journey forward, my hope is that you'll take these enduring traits of companies that have thrived for over a century and make them your own. Embrace their principles of resilience, adaptability, and vision. Recognize your moments of truth and make necessary pivots. Steward your business to transcend generations, ensuring safeguards by planning for succession and cultivating deep relationships. Let the Centurions' stories guide you in crafting your own legacy, one that not only withstands the test of time but evolves and flourishes in an ever-changing world.

The wisdom of the long game is not just about surviving; it's about thriving, innovating, and leaving an indelible mark on the future.

EPILOGUE
YOU ARE THE NEXT CEN

»»»

THE PLAY: *Turn hindsight into foresight.*

In the echoes of our past decisions lie the blueprint for navigating the uncertainties of the future.

We've explored the elements that sustain the longevity of the companies profiled in this book, giving you a powerful framework to appreciate the components of enduring success. I hope this will inspire a new way of looking at a marketplace focused on fast returns, the latest trends, and start-up culture.

Our world faces challenges on multiple fronts—society, politics, foreign policy—all with an increasing velocity of constant change. Whether it's the enterprising founding story of J.M. Smucker, the enduring mission of nonprofits like the Girl Scouts, the resilience of the McKissack family, or the legacy of the Biltmore Estate built by generations of impassioned Vanderbilts, each offers invaluable lessons for coping with such inevitable obstacles.

This framework highlights why such businesses are built to last and also offers a tool for evaluating your organization. These principles can be strategically implemented to ensure that your business is poised to stand the test of time.

By looking back—and thinking ahead—several themes emerge:

Overcoming External Challenges

Companies that have weathered significant external threats, like a global pandemic or disruptive competitors, and emerged stronger are usually built for longevity.

When a company overcomes a crisis, it demonstrates adaptability and strategic foresight. Its response to challenges usually reveals a robust operational framework, a strong leadership team, and an agile mindset.

Designer Gianluca Isaia recognized the exogenous threat that COVID posed to his product line and dramatically revamped it in anticipation of pandemic-wrought fashion upheaval. The end result was a more diverse offering and significantly expanded capabilities of his production facility. When the next crisis comes, Isaia has a broader line of products it can make as needs and interests change. The business is now stronger and more resilient. He showcased an ability to think critically and act swiftly.

When Asheville, North Carolina, was hit by Hurricane Helene in September 2024, the storm forced Biltmore Estate to temporarily close while it addressed damage in the area caused by flooding, impassable roads, and ongoing utility outages whose intensity took the western part of the state by surprise. During this period, Biltmore launched a recovery plan to reopen quickly to help get the local economy moving, and to strengthen resilience against future natural disasters, which included making $2 million immediately available to assist the surrounding community.

Your capacity to strategically pivot in the face of crisis is vital to surviving external shocks to your business. Organizations that achieve long-term sustainability consistently engage in this iterative process of transformation.

Product or Service Reinvention

Demonstrate an inherent aptitude for reinvention.

One secret to the enduring success of Centurion companies lies in their remarkable capacity for reinvention and adaptation. The ability to overhaul a product line and succeed with the next version is not only a significant feat but also a true marker of long-term viability.

In 1815, when steam-powered ships began to replace clipper ships with sails sewn by Loane Brothers seamstresses, founder Joseph Loane resisted the urge to lay off his workers. Instead, he embraced reinvention, leveraging the seamstresses' skills to create hand-stitched commercial awnings that morphed the company into the tent-making business it is today, celebrating over two hundred years of history.

We see such reinvention with newer companies in today's business landscape.

NVIDIA's trajectory mirrors the essence of reinvention with its RIVA 28 chip that rescued the company, ultimately redefining the gaming industry and enabling breakthroughs in AI that would change the world.

Apple also exemplifies the power of reinvention, having adeptly transformed itself multiple times since its 1976 founding. Apple expanded its vision under Steve Jobs, transitioning from a computer manufacturer to a multifaceted technology giant with such groundbreaking products as the iPod, iPhone, and iPad. This capacity for reinvention continued under Tim Cook's leadership, as Apple diversified its ecosystem to include services like Apple Music, Apple TV+, and iCloud. Apple is playing the long game with an eye toward the next one hundred years.

As the business landscape evolves, a commitment to innovation and strategic adaptation positions a company well for long-term success. But sustained relevance relies on its ability to embrace change, making reinvention not just a strategy but a core competency essential for the long run.

Leadership Transitions

Do not put off succession planning. Some companies wait until a leader dies or departs before determining a successor. Start early.

Successfully transitioning from a founder to a new leader, and then from one leader to another, is a strong indicator of stability. Many companies falter at these crucial stages, especially when it comes down to a leader-to-leader transition.

Throughout this book, we've profiled a number of familial succession stories and the challenges that successors face to preserve the company, its family ownership, and family control. Those transitions all looked different:

- Companies like McKissack & McKissack, with Cheryl McKissack Daniel at the helm, are preparing ten years ahead of their leadership transition to a potential nonfamily leader for the first time. Cheryl's commitment to selecting the right leader for the business, rather than merely passing it down to a family member, is likely to set her more-than-a-century-old company on a path to continued long-term success.

- Then there was William Cecil from Biltmore, who turned heads when he made the surprise retirement announcement during a company anniversary celebration in 1995, passing the reins to his thirty-five-year-old son, Bill. The younger Cecil adapted and eventually dedicated Biltmore to formalizing succession with careful planning for future generations.

- In some cases a leader emerges from a crisis. When Salvatore Ferragamo died at sixty-two in 1960, his wife Wanda inherited the business despite having no prior experience. Nevertheless, she embraced her new role with determination, focusing on preparing her children at an early age for leadership roles they'd inherit.

A hierarchical shift inevitably occurs within all long-lasting businesses. It's one that requires careful anticipation and nurturing: passing the torch from founder to new leader, from that leader to the next leader. That's where companies can break down.

Culture

Company culture must be authentic, consistently practiced, and demonstrated through actions, with leaders embodying a strong sense of ownership and accountability to set the tone for the organization.

Culture must be defined and embraced from day one, as it is crucial to an organization's success and serves as the backbone of its values and operations. Understanding the nuances of your culture is essential; without this insight, your company may face significant challenges.

Many long-standing businesses featured in this book have well-defined cultures that enhance their resilience. For example, the Ferragamo family's commitment to their Castiglione del Bosco property illustrated how integral family involvement is to their identity, with members gathering weekly at their winery and resort to foster engagement and dedication to their local community, just as they do global enterprise.

We've looked at personal accountability as a fundamental building block. You'll recall the culture shakeup put in place by James Daunt after he was appointed CEO to save Barnes & Noble, which was closing stores en masse at the time. He instituted the radical idea of empowering employees at the ground level: Booksellers should decide how to sell books. This turned the culture on its ear; previously, people were hired for their retail sales abilities, not necessarily because they understood bookselling.

A company's culture should play a key role in confronting what is not working. The question "What am I tolerating but shouldn't be?" provides the impetus to fix all the things that can go wrong. After being involved with about a hundred companies in my career, I have seen myriad problems, from incompetence to just plain bad luck. But the companies with strong cultures still managed to figure it out.

An upside to this key indicator is that culture is not a rigid, unbending set of rules; it's a living, breathing thing that can be modified. Even if your culture seems to be the root of your company's problems, you have every opportunity to fix it.

Live your culture every day, and that culture is reinforced through repetition. You talk about it all the time. People see your actions, and that they match what you've been preaching. You walk the walk with authenticity. But if you don't do it frequently, it doesn't take.

NEW PLAYS FOR THE NEXT CEN

Private Versus Public Tenure

Businesses that stay private longer may have an edge in longevity. Operating without the pressures of public scrutiny often allows for more focus on long-term strategies over short-term gains.

There appears to be a compelling correlation between a company's longevity and how long it is privately held. Publicly traded companies face constant pressure to deliver short-term results to shareholders, which can lead to a myopic approach that prioritizes quick gains over sustainable growth. In contrast, privately held businesses often prioritize their vision and long-term goals over immediate financial pressures. This focus enables strategic decisions aligned with core values, unswayed by public market scrutiny.

CEOs face tremendous pressure to deliver quarterly results; this is historically driven by Wall Street analysis and shareholder expectations. The popularity of this short-term perspective is surprising, especially considering the evidence isn't just a small trend or two—it's compelling and significant. Most growth companies are staying private much longer, and in some cases, you even wonder if they'll ever go public. It's a fascinating shift.

With the number of public companies declining and private companies staying private longer, understanding and accessing private markets has become essential. Data shows that these organizations are often built for long-term resilience, making private markets a significant driver of wealth creation in today's economy.

Family offices, such as ours at Cresset, are evolving their investment approach, almost an alternative private equity. It's more about long-duration capital—long-term thinking and Centurion-style investing for companies with staying power. This is a significant shift, one that supports companies that can last for generations.

Private companies, with their unique structures, are well suited to embrace a long-term perspective, possessing the flexibility to make strategic decisions for their futures. Consequently, the choice between staying private or going public can significantly shape a company's capacity to innovate, adapt, and endure over time.

Organic Growth

In an era where quick wins and acquisitions dominate headlines, those that prioritize organic growth are not merely surviving—they are laying the foundation for enduring success.

Businesses focused on short-term profits through mass acquisitions, or "roll-ups," tend to be shortsighted. The nature of the roll-up puts you in the deal business. Your business centers on doing deals, finding targets, persuading them to sell, structuring a deal, negotiating the deal, diligence, closing, integration, then . . . *boom*! Move on to the next one.

When that's at the core of what you do, it's not longevity that defines your DNA—it's the dealmaking. Your company likely embodies that transactional mindset.

Healthy organic growth is a key indicator of a business with potential for longevity. Once that's in place, acquisitions should be thoughtful and culturally compatible. By contrast, roll-ups are more of a quick-win strategy for financial sponsors. Real value stems from sustained and natural growth, which makes a company much more attractive to those it seeks to acquire. The business also is in a great position to pursue strategic acquisitions that fit well and create long-term value.

The Centurion companies I've talked to have accomplished organic growth in a variety of ways:

- Whirlpool, Harley-Davidson, and torta-making company Inés Rosales built core products known for their quality and long-term market presence. They ascribe to the "do one thing well" philosophy. These brands cultivated growth through a strong brand identity (Harley-Davidson) or by leveraging customer loyalty and feedback to drive innovation (Whirlpool, Inés Rosales).

Freedman Seating fostered organic growth by heeding the rapidly evolving nature of the industry it serves, mass transportation.

Cresset started with a loyal base of family and friends as its first clients. It achieved organic growth through word of mouth and authentic connections.

Avy and I came from outside the family office industry, but we had been clients for decades. This gave us a unique perspective on what was missing in the market and what we wanted for ourselves. The initial spark for Cresset came from deep customer insight—understanding their needs. From there, the way we approached growth was driven by these insights as we constantly tested and refined our solutions for how to meet market demand.

We also followed a clear playbook, telling our first ten employees that we were embarking on a one-hundred-year journey together, building a culture rooted in organic growth. And our long game continues . . .

ACKNOWLEDGMENTS
WHAT THE FUTURE HOLDS

»»»

The lessons that lead to longevity are timeless.

I'd like to express my gratitude to the amazing companies I've encountered—those who've shared their stories on and off the record. As I've gathered information, read different accounts, and met families, all have contributed to the thinking behind this book.

I think back to the moment I picked up that newspaper in Baltimore and saw Loane Brothers listed as one of the nation's oldest companies. That's what sparked my curiosity—how did they make it this long? That moment, and many others like it, ultimately led to my passion for chronicling the secrets to success of companies built to stand the test of time.

The criteria outlined in this playbook serve as a blueprint. The wisdom embedded within these pages, drawn from the lessons of Centurion companies, embodies a commitment to longevity and adaptability.

These learnings would have greatly benefitted my father, who navigated the challenges of his Santa Claus rental business for over fifty-seven years. While he may not have achieved Centurion status, Gordon Becker remains my beacon of inspiration for the entrepreneurial spirit that propelled me on this quest to uncover and share the essence of Centurion businesses.

As you embark on your own journey through this playbook, it is my fervent hope that you too will find inspiration in these stories and principles, empowering you to cultivate a legacy that endures and thrives in the face of change.

Together, let's honor the values that endure and build a future where our businesses don't just survive but thrive for generations.

That is the power we hold—to create a legacy of lasting prosperity, together.